KUNDALINI
from
HELL
to
HEAVEN

Wisdom From The Completed Journey Of Ganga Karmokar

Ganga Karmokar
('Swami-G')

KUNDALINI
From Hell to Heaven

Published by Zen Way Centre

ISBN: 0-9777456-0-0

First edition 2002.
Second edition Sept 2006

Beyond thought there is no division... Experience is direct... you are ONE within whatever is appearing to happen...All moves through the Constant as transient happenings... But the Constant makes the viewing of the transient as a mysterious, 'wonder-full' happening of Self...

There is nothing that is to be learned, it is more a process of letting go... you do not gain anything... how can you gain what has always been and will always be Reality? You only drop the illusions of truth and surrender all the so-called knowledge you have gained... only then are the illusions dispelled and the Light of Truth remains... and Self is KNOWN... Beyond mind, beyond time, beyond body, beyond the transient realm of Maya to the Constant - which IS the Self Alone...

Ganga Karmokar

Dedication

Namaste, readers. This book is dedicated to all those who put me on the path the Self-Realization: to Father Blighton who started the process, to AC Bhaktivedanta Swami who taught me the Bhakti path and told me that Self-Realization would be reached in this lifetime, and to Rajiv Misra, my final Guru who had the courage to confront me with what was needed rather than with what was wanted. Each of them had an important part to play within my journey and each remains with me in a very real way. For the Truth is, we are all One beyond division.

This book is also dedicated to those who share their stories and paths here and for those who are yet to come. Hopefully this book will serve to inform the health care profession who will encounter many kundalini cases in the years to come. The truth of the matter is that those in the fields of psychology and psychiatry and general healthcare physicians have a long way to go before understanding just what the process of kundalini is and how to best serve those with whom they come in contact.

Thank you to Jeff Belyea for making the first printing possible and for those who have helped with this second printing. A special thank you to Maggie Corbin for designing the cover for this new edition.[1]

It is my prayer that each person who completes the kundalini path successfully will go on and share the way to completion with others. In this way the world will enter into Peace and balance one person at a time.

Shanti om .g.

---

[1] For Graphic design: corbinm@sover.net .

Note on the Text

"...there are no adequate words...you cannot describe That Which Is or the Constant or God beyond Form or the Source...it is impossible..."

Ganga Karmokar

Prior to undertaking the editing of this text, I was advised by a Swami to make as few alterations as possible. This is a difficult task for an editor preparing a text for public discrimination. What reason could there be for this advice and to what degree should I follow it? The reply was that the author is one who has "completed the journey - who resides in stillness". The words within this book flow from that stillness - and this flow pays no attention to convention. To alter the words is to interfere with the flow.

You will notice within this book that Ganga Karmokar's sentences are often dispersed with '...' - this denotes a pause, an opportunity to allow that which is behind the words to come forth. Ganga Karmokar speaks from the stillness - not from 'rational' thought. Her words here need not be grasped or clung to, rather simply allowed to flow.

Some of you will discover, as I did, that a sense of peace will filter through and a subtle flowing through the heart begins to move unhindered.

J M Hale, Editor

CONTENTS

CONTENTS (continued)

PART 1

The Truth
Of
Your Being

Why This Book Was Written

Namaste and welcome to all who find this book. Having traversed the kundalini journey from start to finish, I knew that a book had to be written and I promised that whatever knowledge I gleaned would be shared most openly. Why? Simply because kundalini is so misunderstood. I would like to share the knowledge I have discovered through this most difficult experience.

During my journey, I searched for a teacher or a guide and found nothing except those with theories who had read some books or were teaching methods of yoga. None of these people were able to answer the questions that were ringing in my mind or were able to give any definitive advice as to how to proceed. Teachings regarding chakras and energy fields, yogic postures and theories did nothing except to confuse the issue.

Doctors and mental health professionals wanted to label and categorize. Tests were run, pills were given, diagnosis after diagnosis appeared. With each new prescription there was simply more toxicity, while no help was forthcoming. The health care realm simply made the process even more unbearable.

This will not be a book on energies, chakras, theories, etc. as there are enough of those lining the shelves of bookstores. This book will focus on my story and the stories of others, along with knowledge from one who has transcended the path. There are answers to questions that are being asked every day. Finally, we have the tools and ways to navigate the path to completion.

Thank you for coming and sharing this great unfolding adventure. The world is indeed changing one person at a time. Each who completes the process successfully will find true Liberation and the Peace Which Passes All Understanding. It IS possible.

So here we go on the great kundalini adventure from hell to heaven and the path through consciousness…

shanti om .g.

Ego, Bondage and Illusions
Of Truth

All of our emotional bondages are created and held in place by that which is known as ego. Ego is the belief that we are these bodies, emotions, and thoughts. Therefore when anything goes against any of these systems we hold it to be an assault against our persona. Depending on our belief system and identity which is already in place the disturbance can be mildly irritating to downright devastating. If we encountered a traumatic situation where there was a belief that impending death was just around the corner then that trauma may be re-run again and again in the psyche, creating even more pain and perceived trauma. But there is a way to short-circuit these illusions of truth. For anything that is not liberating is not Truth at all but an illusion of truth. It is these illusions that we will address. How are they created and what sustains them? And if they are illusions how can we move beyond them? If we are not this ego structure then what are we? How can peace of mind be attained and preserved? Where do we begin and where will this search end? Believe it or not that which you fear the most can be that which liberates you in the end. The largest perceived fear can be the greatest liberator. Please bear with me in this.

Right now you are probably thinking that this woman has a serious screw loose somewhere! And if I were in your place, I would probably think the same thing right about now. But I have been where you are and have escaped the seemingly concrete fears and thought constructions and emotional baggage which kept me bound for many years. I have walked the path and therefore can speak from the position of direct experiential knowledge and not hearsay. All I will speak of has been acquired by direct experience. I do not have a Ph.D. but rather a direct knowledge of truth, as it is. It is this truth that I wish to share with you today.

Conditionings

From the moment we are born, the conditionings begin. And the conditions of life are set. We are born into this world with a body. Some bodies are seen as perfect and some as flawed. We are born into a family. Some are glad at the arrival and perhaps some are not. All of these things begin to create the conditionings and conditions of our lives. The views of our parents and society and friends all have an impact on our thought structures and perceptions. These all come together to create our basic outlook on life and what we hold to be truth. These all create our perceptions of truth.

If you are supported and told you are smart then you have confidence in whatever you do. While on the other hand, if you are always told you are stupid and ugly then this will color your world and view of reality. This colors your thoughts of who you perceive yourself to be, along with all the other events in life which also color and interplay within your reality framework. One person whom has always been sheltered within a loving family will see the world as a kind and beneficial beautiful place to be. Whereas one whom has come from a harsh and abusive environment will see the world colored as a place to be continually on guard. Then there are events which unfold in everyone's life which will skew even these basic belief systems.

Holding onto the past

Now you begin to see just how much the conditionings create our basic view of reality as we know it - or 'think' it to be. With this out of the way we begin right where you are at this moment in time. The first thing we do is to look at the fact that the past is past. So if you are rerunning the tapes of the past let's look at the fact that by running them over and over you can change nothing. All you are doing is reinforcing past nonsense that is keeping you bound in one form or another. If it were not keeping you bound, it would have passed right out of your awareness. For whatever reason you perceive, you are continually holding on to this perception - whether slight or hurt or trauma. And you have to admit it, is not doing anything constructive in your life.

'What if' factor

Now let's look at the other waste of energy which we continually find ourselves involved in. And this is the 'what if' factor. Trying to live in the future just never works as the only place that you can ever truly live is in the Present Moment of Now. So what is happening when you are running the past tapes and the 'what if' tapes? In essence, you are passing life by…You are only existing! You are not living at all…Life is in a holding pattern. Continually circling around and around. And the more you feed the past and the 'what ifs', the more they grow into unmanageable cyclones of wasted energy and efforts. You are only attempting to deal with a change, something which is already gone. It lives only within your illusion of truth. And the conflict is there because of the ego identification with the body and emotions and thoughts. And in Truth you are none of these things.

So now you ask, "where do I go from here!?" And from here I say it is time you found out the Truth of who and what you really are and who you are not. Once you know at long last just what comprises your Being, then the rest of that which is illusion will just drop away of its own accord. When these things are no longer given any energy then they will just dissipate into the vapors of unreality that they are. Like a drop of dew evaporates in the sunlight, these illusions will dissipate under the light of Truth.

Are you ready to begin the never-ending adventure? Are you ready to begin to really live life to the fullest? To grab and rest in the freedom which is just waiting for you? It is ALWAYS there and has always been there. It is only your own blinders which keep you from seeing it. Is your fear that you are nothing and nobody? Is your great fear that of death and that you will cease to be? Let us examine these fears and see what comes out of them.

Freedom to Be

Let us proceed to look at what is transient. What is it about you that comes and goes? When you peel away the layers of the transient, what is it that remains? When you come to what remains you will come to the truth of your being! You will see that there was nothing to fear and that there is only freedom that remains. Won't that be a lovely thing to remain? Just FREEDOM to BE. The freedom of knowing that you are the unbound truth of existence, that all you perceived was just an illusion of bondage and fear which never had any reality at all - except that which you yourself gave it.

So are you ready to unravel all the fears and thoughts and emotions that have kept you tied on the wheel of karma? Are you ready to let go of the desires that keep you bound to the wheel of birth and death? For it is not the actions which keep you on the wheel of karma, going around and around. It is the thought and intent of the actions. And it is the re-actions of the actions which come against you which once again keep you bound to the wheel of birth and death. Just going around and around in the never-ending spiral called life and death...birth and rebirth...We keep circling through the same old patterns again and again until we can break the cycle. In each life we will draw the same patterns to ourselves, keep creating the same illusions of truth until we can break free and can see them for what they are. And once we see through them, the pattern will drop and we move onward to a new experience. Look at your life and see what patterns keep coming up again and again. Now let's walk through the door of knowledge to liberation and the Freedom which awaits...

The Truth of Your Being

What is mind?

What is mind? Is it a physical thing? Let us first look here. What is the mind comprised of? Is not the mind comprised of thoughts? And just what are thoughts? Are they some concrete existence? NO! Thoughts come and go like waves on the sea. First one thought is there and then another and so on and so on. One arises and falls and then the next, and so on infinitum. But there can only be one thought that makes its appearance at a time.

Sometimes these thoughts will start in a whirlpool one after another just going around and around until you are dizzy and disoriented just from the sheer continued motion and circling around and around. But look at it again. Even though there are certain thought patterns which keep appearing and cycling, they ultimately come and go. If they come and go, they are not concrete in nature but fluid. And like waves on the ocean they can appear like a ripple or with enough energy, can appear as a tidal wave pulling you out into a sea of emotion and fear and despair only because they have touched upon an illusion of truth. They come and rock your world, creating waves in your reality.

Let us continue on in this search until we uncover the Reality that cannot be shaken. When you come to the Truth you will be set free as the Truth always IS and is the basis for ALL of creation. ALL has proceeded from Truth - is sustained by Truth - and will once again return to truth. Illusions being what they are in the end must disappear; when the illusion is uncovered it ceases to be!

So we see that mind is comprised of individual thoughts which come and go. One thought manifesting at a time. So mind is not concrete in nature. Mind is an illusion. Mind has no substance. Let us move on now to thought.

What is thought?

What is thought? Thought also has no concrete nature. So exactly what and where do thoughts manifest from? They have no substance. They arise from nowhere and return to nowhere. So why is so much importance given to something which comes and goes from nowhere to nowhere? When it leaves our awareness and perception, where does it go? It only has life while in the framework of our perceptions. When these thoughts float into our awareness what happens? We give it life by then ascribing emotions to it. When a thought comes in if you look at it and dwell on it does it not elicit an emotion? So this emotion gives the thought life for that moment in time.

Let us follow the emotion. Emotions come and go. They are something that are particular to you alone. No one else feels your emotion but you. Others may see your reaction to the emotion but the emotion itself is yours alone.

Is emotion a concrete thing? No! You cannot have an emotion that lives independently on its own. You are the one that gives it life. Your attention to it gives it energy and life. And once again emotions come and go like the waves of an ocean. In and out. High tide and low tide. And since they are transient in nature they are not the reality of your Being. They are but ripples on the sea of Consciousness. One emotion arises and is there for some time until replaced by another emotion. Once again they are only waves and ripples without any concrete form. Emotions are created and held in place by mind and thought. And we have already seen that mind and thought have no substance and are only passing illusions. And these illusions create and sustain all the Ill-lusions that keep us bound.

So let us review. We know that we are not the physical body. If you see something, are you that which is being seen? Is the body that which is watching itself? Nor can we be the mind which is created by thoughts. Nor are we the individual thoughts. Nor are we the conglomerate of thoughts. If we are neither of these then it follows that we also cannot be the emotions which the mind and thoughts create and sustain. And isn't our whole persona just made up and held together by all these illusions of mind, thought and emotion?

So let us keep going and seeing just what is left? My goodness do I even exist at all? I think it is safe to say yes, you do exist - just not the way you thought and perceived! So when we take away the body, the mind, the thoughts, the emotions - just what is left?

The Truth of your Being

How do you know you have thoughts? How do you know you dream at night? Or that there were no dreams? It is because of Conscious Awareness! You are this Conscious Awareness...It sees the thoughts...But It is not the thoughts. It is aware of the emotions. But It is NOT the emotions. It is aware of form but It is not form. It is Not concrete in nature yet clearly It IS...

You are in fact No-Body...and you are No-Thing...You are Awareness - Energy - Vibration - Truth - and Bliss...and these are eternal in nature...They are that which creates and sustains existence. All form, while appearing and disappearing is created by these alone - and therefore always exists. The form may change but it is eternal for it never was the concrete illusion of truth which we see. See beyond the form to the Formless... See beyond the illusions of truth to the Reality of Truth.

Now let us continue onward. Now we come to the point of putting all this together. Since we are in reality Conscious Awareness and Energy and Vibration and Truth and Bliss, just what thought or emotion or physical happening can touch us? None can truly touch out essence! All of the perceived traumas and hurts have happened only to this body...and you are not this body.

This is how we diffuse the bondage. When the pain comes again go into it. Go to the root. There is nothing to. Go into the fear fully and see that when you reach the end of it that it will just dissipate as it is only comprised of illusions of truth. When thoughts come and go just see them as passing clouds with no substance. Do not give them form and life...Let them come and go like waves on the ocean. Instead of being carried away by a tidal wave get in the boat and float downstream and enjoy the ride.

When you drop the mind of thoughts and illusions you will reach the still waters of the Peace which passes all understanding. You will be the everlasting waters. You will not thirst again. You alone create the fears and bondages of life. And you have the power to let all of them go. Just go into the illusion and it will dissipate before your very eyes. You will not cease to exist nor will you find more bondage. What you will find is the doorway to freedom. You have never truly been born nor have you died. You are beyond these forms and plays of life. As all this is created by mind and thought. So go beyond all these illusions to what and who you really are...

Live life to the fullest! You are here to explore and be Existence. So drop all the self-doubts and illusions of truth that keep you going around and around. You are Life... You are Bliss...Drop the illusive mind and thought. You are Sat - Chit - Anand.[2] This is the Truth of your Being...And what in reality can touch or harm This Truth?

Nothing at all.

---

[2] Truth – Awareness - Bliss

PART 2

My Life
and
Kundalini Journey

My Life and Kundalini Journey
Part 1 – Kundalini Awakening
(fears, phenomena)

The long kundalini journey began in 1969. I was in an esoteric Christian order called Holy Order of Man. I was living in the main house premises. One night while attending the evening prayers, I was kneeling at the altar when Father Blighton laid his hands upon my head to bless me as was the regular custom. Suddenly, a large bolt of gold light shot through my body and it felt as if it had nailed me to the floor. It was four to five inches across - absolutely gold, it was like being struck by lightning.

Father Blighton just smiled and said, "You have just entered into the first stage of enlightenment." I must comment here that while it was appealing and ego-boosting to hear those words that night, I now must say that I do not see 'stages' of enlightenment. There are shifts that may occur though during the process along the way and these will be discussed later.

From the moment of this kundalini awakening for approximately three days in duration there was the entering into what I *now* know was a Sarvikalpa Samadhi state. At the time I only knew that there was a connection to all things in the universe and yet it was being watched like watching a play. If I had died in that moment it would be no loss for all the world was at peace and within God. This first opening experience after a time lessened and faded while colors began to be seen. Auras were seen around the crosses in the chapel. The cross on the altar had a glow of purple around it, and the one on the wall had a gold glow and aura. There was still at that time somewhat of a feeling of a dream state.

During the time in the Order, a stage of praying and manifesting and trusting the universe was entered. It seemed that whatever was prayed for would in some way shape or form appear. I left the Order not too long afterwards due to some jealousy that after such a short time I had moved up to wearing the blue cinching that pointed to the fact of the kundalini awakening in progress. From there I went into the military service and during that time developed PTSD. It is necessary for me to point out that those experiences are quite different from the kundalini experiences that arose alongside it.

The kundalini took a gentle back seat and seemed to settle for about ten years, no doubt it was still working in a subtle way but was not perceptible in a life-altering way during that time.

I spent some time with AC Bhaktivedanta. This gave me a good understanding of the Bhakti path. I did not take initiation but did have a personal interview whereby he said, "You will reach Realization within this lifetime". It was not my lifepath to stay in ISKON[3] and so I left and spent the next years in contemplation, studying the bible, and in internal prayer for wisdom and to 'know the truth'.

One night I decided to sit down and meditate. The moment that a focus was directed inward, the kundalini shot up and became quite active. It was like having liquid fire racing up the spinal column. Thus began the kundalini journey in earnest, and it continued from that point to its completion in 1999. This time there was no bliss of Samadhi but simply the feeling that one would spontaneously combust at any moment.

Upon going to sleep, I was awakened by the sound of hundreds of birds all chirping at once. This made further sleep impossible. When I complained to my husband at the time he said, "There are no birds - it is midnight." I argued with him, "Don't you hear them? They are so loud I cannot sleep!" Looking out of the window, I saw he was right. The inner sounds of Nad had awakened.[4] Later I found that Saint Theresa had also written of experiencing the sounds of hundreds of birds. Many Christian Saints experienced kundalini awakenings. It is my feeling that due to what is experienced, especially at Enlightenment, it would be impossible for them to fully write about what happened. To admit the final Truth of God and Reality would have been tantamount to heresy during their lifetimes. Therefore the Christian Saints' voyages through the kundalini experience were always couched in some secrecy.

From this further awakening, the journey became more difficult and tenuous at best. I had no idea of kundalini at this

---

[3] Krishna movement

[4] (This is the sound that occurs as the kundalini moves through the Nadi systems and cellular body).

point. I only knew that something drastic was happening. Fear mounted and the ongoing heat and continued sounds and feelings grew. I had no idea where to look and went to a hospital where it was suggested that I was either schizophrenic or had temporal lobe epilepsy. After an MRI revealed there was nothing abnormal within the brain itself, the other testing began. I was put on anti-seizure medications which only clouded my thinking and made me toxic. They did nothing to alter the mounting range of experiences that were encountered.

Encountering the rising list of phenomena was no small feat. During this time I would be sitting in a chair and the body would be jerked so strongly inside that I felt as if a large earthquake had happened. I would ask, "Did you feel that earthquake?" Of course the answer was "no". The heat now intensified into a feeling as if the whole nervous system in the body was short-circuiting. Upon lying down, it sounded as if someone was close to my ear and said forcefully, "HAH!" Needless to say I almost jumped out of my skin. Looking around, there was no one there. Next, while sitting in the living room, it felt as if someone was running their fingers through my hair, creating a tingling feeling.

The medical community while evaluating me for schizophrenia and temporal lobe epilepsy began to do EEG's. The first showed an altered state of consciousness. It was not consistent with temporal lobe epilepsy however. They tried medication after medication all of which simply made me once again more toxic and did nothing to intervene in the still mounting phenomena. Finally it was concluded that I did not have schizophrenia. (There was no hearing of voices that were outwards or schizophrenic paranoia of that type. I was also having the PTSD flashbacks and fears at this time, but they were distinct and separate from the kundalini experience.) Sexual activity became unbearable. The energy felt out of control at times.

Then came the fears and 'fight or flight' feelings. Internal lights were seen that began to revolve in my vision. Then a blue light appeared. It was always there in my waking vision in the corner of the room. The light was always seen like a blue pearl on the right hand side of the visionary space. It did not leave and was there for months. At this point, receiving no help from the medical community, I began to search. I finally found the book by Gopi Krishna[5] and what it contained mirrored my experiences.

PART 2 - Dreams, Siddhis, Bliss

Dreams of snakes
During quite a reasonably active period of kundalini there was a dream in which a taxi pulled up alongside me. I opened the door and found the taxi was filled with snakes. (The body was indeed filled with the kundalini manifestation) In another dream I was walking on a boardwalk-type sidewalk when right behind me a large snake appeared. I flew in the sky and it followed me. I landed on a rooftop.

Dreams of fire
A large fire that consumed everything in its path was charging behind me. I just kept trying to outrun it to keep it from consuming me. (During this time the kundalini manifestation was including extreme heat).

Journeying
I was standing along a road when a buckboard wagon stopped. There were three people seated. They asked if I wanted to go with them. I saw the girl turn my way, her hair parted on her forehead revealing a third eye. On the side of the buckboard it was carved the name *Argonaut.* I decided to go with them.

Past life
This was a past-life encounter dream which was extremely lucid and real. I was a monk that was participating in a ceremony where the demons were invited to feed upon your flesh. It became quite real and I lost my mind. (At the time I knew nothing of Tibetan ceremonies called 'Chod', but indeed found that this does exist and it also explained certain happenings within this lifetime that were manifesting). Later, while in India, a Tibetan Lama did my chart which not surprisingly confirmed that my last life was in fact, as a monk.

Symbolism
I was riding a white horse which ran into a church, upon entering I looked up and the whole roof blew off. (Indeed part of

---

[5] Living with Kundalini, *Gopi Krishna, Shambala Dragon Edts.*

the process of kundalini is to take all of your concepts of religion and blow them out.)
There were many more vivid dreams of snakes and vehicles; many more dreams of a symbolic nature along the way.

During the time of the vivid dreams and feeling as if the whole nervous system was short-circuiting, a flame pattern appeared in the center of the chest. This lasted for a good month. Then one day while driving, suddenly it was as if someone poured a glass of ice water right inside the chest where this flame pattern was. The pattern receded a few days later. Also at this time, all the senses became so heightened that when going to San Francisco I could barely navigate walking through some of the buildings there. Due to the earthquake factor some of the new buildings are built on roller systems and to me it was like walking on a swinging bridge.

Then siddhis began to emerge and the ability to feel everything that was happening in another person's body came to the forefront. At that time the ability to heal also became pronounced. Energy work was not something 'learned' but something simply 'known' totally - within an instant. Kriyas happened spontaneously wherein yoga positions and hand mudras which had never been studied would flow. Eventually they ended after a period of time. None of this was intentional in nature - it simply happened. Other happenings included driving and suddenly finding the conscious awareness was above the trees looking all the way to the ocean. When I realized what had happened the consciousness snapped back into the physical form.

Throughout this time the hospital was still doing more and more tests. Finally I was monitored for two weeks straight to rule out temporal lobe epilepsy. A PET scan was carried out to test the chemical reactions of the brain. There was no organic imbalance. The mental health diagnosis was put in many brackets from borderline personality disorder to manic depressive with schizo-affective tendencies etc. etc. etc. The problem with this was that I was not caught in the illusions and the visionary phenomena that were occurring. I did not lose any connection with so-called reality - however, I was seriously beginning to question my sanity.

The sounds of internal Nad changed with time. Things that were at one time calming took on sinister overtones and irrational fears over took me. I feared that this was something 'evil' and that if I touched my daughter she might become possessed. It was mental torture. The thoughts came unbidden. When trying to pray blasphemies would come to mind. More and more fears mounted. At one point I could feel a malevolent energy surround me, and I curled on the floor with my hands covering my head.

I finally learned to face the fear. Fighting it only made it grow. Any attention made it grow. Finally there was nothing left to do but to surrender one hundred per cent to God. I did once more. The terror came and then it passed. I survived and it came no more.

Over the years the heat and feeling of short circuiting continued. I became completely sensitive to the energy of others around me and to the city itself. One time whilst walking into a New Age fair, I had to leave as black dots swam in front of my vision while a feeling of disconnection overwhelmed me.

Eventually I had money to go to India. This was after thirty years of suffering. It was there that all unraveled and the completion took place. My Guru, Rajiv Misra pulled out from beneath me, what little rug remained. This triggered my questioning of the self-identity directly.

Then there was a mystical happening, experienced as a pure gold lingam of light and the eternal sound of OM. There was no beginning or no end to the eternal sound of OM which penetrated the universe. It reverberated through the body, was felt to the very core and was the core. While lying in bed one night, I suddenly sat bolt upright and *knew* "I" was not the body/mind/emotions. In that instant all of the trauma faded away for it happened to the physical form alone and "I" am not this body. It was like being born again. Feeling white as snow.

> *I humbly bow*
> *and kiss the Lotus feet*
> *of my Guru*
> *For he has taken me*
> *from darkness to light.*
> *He has shattered*
> *the world, and has*

given me eternity.
He has cast sin,
body and mind
into the darkness;
and only sinless
Truth eternal remains...

There was yet further to go...from this point "I" started to lose body awareness more and more. Sometimes the body felt like a puppet that the consciousness was attempting to move. On some occasions not too successfully. On other occasions it was like being a large bubble just floating along. Then the Bliss emerged again...but this time the bliss was more overwhelming:

What is this world compared to this Bliss,
compared to this Bliss
compared to this Bliss of Self Divine...
There is nothing to see compared to this Bliss
compared to this Bliss
compared to this Bliss of Self Divine...
there is nothing to touch (compared to this Bliss)
there is nothing to feel (compared to this Bliss)
there is nothing to hear (compared to this Bliss)
there is nothing to taste (compared to this Bliss)
there is nothing to do (compared to this Bliss)
there is nothing to be (compared to this Bliss)
there is nothing to speak but
only to BE - but only to BE -
but only to BE this Bliss of Self Divine...
to BE the "Self Divine"...

PART 3 - End of Kundalini Journey

I continued to question and contemplate. The mind by this point was entering a stillness and silence. My teacher had left India and was in the United States. I continued my sadhana and questioning. I knew that still this was not Realization. There was still an 'I' that was experiencing. I sat down on the banks of the Ganges and finally the last great fear of death rose up like a black suffocating void that sat there waiting to swallow me up...I 'knew' that something would not survive and yet also knew that what remained was to surrender totally to know that which I had been searching for so long. I surrendered and was sucked into Source, a Nirvikalpa Samadhi beyond the five senses, and on the way, that which was termed "I" was seen to never have existed. There was no "I" as such. There was ONLY Source the Primal Essence: the infinite Pregnant Void, Total Intellect without knowledge, Original Mind Pure and Undefiled, This Source that is Eternal in Nature that was never born - never died. Coming back, all this was KNOWN.

The kundalini ended in that moment beyond time and movement. Shakti or energy and movement into form merged with the Unchanging Unlimited Source the Primal Nature that is ever beyond division. Spit out the other side was a new Being. There was no feeling of reality to the universe at that time...this world was for months simply a dream state and no more and no less. Eventually integration came wherein the world is seen as totally empty in nature and therefore ever ONE and non-dual. That in the end is the residing awareness. Movement simply happens. All is now spontaneous flow. The mind rests within stillness. There is nothing to attach to and vairagya or detachment is a normal state. It is not something clung to or developed. It simply IS.

The kundalini raises not its head any longer in display - for the world is known for what it is. With Source being its full Formless or its apparent diversity of knowing: it matters not for it is One and the same...

Enlightenment Within Daily Life

Taken from an interview:

Q: *If you were Enlightened, what would be different?*
G: Nothing is different...
Q: *What do you think your experience of Reality would be?*
G: The world moves forward as it is...but instead of seeing the diversity as the ultimate, the One underneath it all is rested in...Like the ocean, reality or Maya is simply the surface waves of moving consciousness - Shakti, which manifests the underlying Ocean of Consciousness into a limited visible form...what is beneath and around and within that form is simply the same consciousness which comprises the Whole of the Ocean...But in the calm of the depths you know the vastness instead of the limited...
Q: *It's been something that has been on my mind for some time now... Would it be vastly different?*
G: Yes and no...the paradoxical answer...no, the world moves the same...but what has changed is your relationship to the world...no longer caught up in the play thereof... being in the world but not of it - you remain going through the motions of everyday life...but while the surface 'personality' may be seen to be involved within the everyday emotions and foibles, underneath, within you, the reality is a steady calm... nothing moves the center...the waves still appear to manifest on the surface but you are absorbed in the deep...where there is no movement...that state within is utter calm...
Q: *Would it be an experience? Or would it be an abiding feeling?*
G: Everything from then on becomes pure experience...No judging nor categorizing...no separation from the experience at hand - it is entered into fully...The feeling is one of continued wholeness - calm - the peace which passes all understanding...the difference is between one that gulps a cheap wine versus a connoisseur which smells the fragrance...and feels the warmth and gets everything out of the experience of the moment...not judging it good nor bad but simply the experience of the Eternal Moment which is

ever in flux and fluid within the transient and stable being that it is never ending, eternally ONE...

Q: *How would you know, what would you expect to have happen?*

G: hahahaha that is just it...you expect Nothing and accept all things...it just becomes an unfolding...there is no longer expectation...nor anxiety... nor desire...just a centered calm in the midst of moving consciousness...non-moving awareness...

Q: *It would probably help to know the territory, what do you believe you'd possess or know that you don't possess or know now?*

G: You possess no longer anything...even the so-called knowledge that you held and treasured recedes...all is pulled away...all drifts away...but what has changed is the Perception...instead of living within the noise and seeking the silence...you are the Silence and the sound rises from there...instead of being within the play...there is simply the pregnant emptiness wherefrom manifestation appears and then once again recedes into...it is the Perception that is changed...instead of the motion you are the stillness...the motion continues on the surface but no longer moves the depths of Being...

PART 3

Shared Stories

Shared Stories ...

Illness, Medical Misdiagnosis. No-Self State.
J.R., Seattle, Washington

From the age of seventeen I've had strange experiences. I've never felt quite in my body and was constantly troubled by intrusive thoughts, depression, strange bodily sensations and anxiety. I began meditating after my son was born, hoping initially to find some breaks in this suffering and not transmit my fears and depression to him. I had a deep, sustaining desire to be free so that I could be made useful to the world. This desire was and still is deep, profound and unwavering.

I had no idea what kundalini was and was not at all prepared for the experiences to follow.

During the first year of meditating, I'd have days where it felt as if a tight cap was being taken off my head. My perceptions felt loose and airy. One day I started giggling to myself while standing in line in a bank. Another day after an emotional period of sobbing, my hands went up on their own in prayer. I was surprised by this. It settled me immediately and I stopped crying. Four more years followed. I recall one day, after taking a walk, I felt funny and light headed. I went to lie down. When I shut my eyes, everything appeared white. There was a white broom sweeping out my brain. Sweeping every cobweb, every corner, every speck of dust. Without words, a question was posed to me; "Do you want to come in?" My reply was, "Only if it's right and good". At this point my intentions were revealed and I knew they were pure.

A year or so passed. One day I had a strange sense that I was very tall. I'm tall anyway, but when I looked down toward the ground, I felt so very high up. It almost made me feel dizzy. I began having dry heaves. All day for months, the dry heaves continued. Sometimes I'd throw up. I thought I had the flu or something, but something felt different about it. My mind would drift far away very easily and I would shiver as if I was cold. When I tried to eat, I had a hard time swallowing due to feeling ill and my body would quake. I began dropping things out of my hands. My hands would just open on their own and then the pain started. All of my muscles tightened and stiffened in pain. Even my armpits hurt. When I walked, my legs were stiff and I felt as if a force was pushing me at the hips. I began crumbling psychologically as well. I would weep and weep for hours as if my life hung by a thread. I felt as if there was nothing to hold onto, as if I were being swept away by a strong current out to who knows where. It felt terribly cruel. I was extremely worried about my son and his well being. I went on crying everyday. It hurt to walk. At night anxiety would rush up through my chest and it felt as if a great pressure pinned me to the bed. Meanwhile a horror show was running through my mind. Violent images, terror. Virtually everything that scared me arose in my brain. Suicidal thoughts followed this. I couldn't work, eat or care for my child. I remember one night, my tongue went numb and began to twitch all through the night. The next day my mind was blank. I wasn't able and had no desire to lift my head off the pillow. I had visions of suicide.

I had been to many doctors. I told my story over and over again. Not one had an understanding of what was happening to me. I was sent home with no help or direction. (This was after all physical illnesses were ruled out. I had much blood work done. I saw several neurologists and had an MRI of the brain and spinal cord. All results were normal.)

On my journey through this, I ended up on a psychiatric ward for three weeks. This is not the best place to be for people going through kundalini, but unfortunately many are routed here due to exhausting other options.

Most of the staff on the psych ward were kind to me. The patients were doped up and many walked very stiff due to side effects from their meds, so my walk fit right in. Some of the patients received electroconvulsive therapy or ECT. I befriended one patient, an older lady who received ECT. When she returned from her treatments, she didn't know my name or hers. She couldn't remember anything. She didn't even recognize me. This was troubling to me because I felt vague and blank myself. Fortunately, I had a room to myself in the ward for awhile. I wasn't sleeping at all.

One night, my legs began to burn terribly and feel like needles were stabbing into them. I recall wrapping sheets from the other bed tightly around my legs. I wrapped and wrapped and tried to rest again. My mind was panicked. In the morning, feeling quite unrested, still laying down, I watched my arm travel on its own from the pillow to my hip. I was horrified. I got up nauseous and dizzy.

Every morning at about seven, a team of psychiatrists entered my room. I told them, "My body is so hot. It's moving on its own. I would sob and sob in my hospital gown. I was given Paxil at the time (an anti-depressant) and Klonopin (an anti-anxiety). Both medications ended up being very helpful to me. I'm happy to say I'm not on these medications now, but not ashamed that I needed them for a while. I continued to have a hard time just walking around. I would attend the craft group and try to focus my mind on making some clay figure. I tried desperately to just pay attention to the movements of my shaky hands.

My diagnosis was major depression, Obsessive Compulsive Disorder for the intrusive thoughts and a little Post Traumatic Stress Disorder mixed in. I remember one very insensitive psychiatrist suggested I undergo ECT. Of course this horrified me. She said, "Your depression just isn't getting any better".

I eventually ended up at home again with every responsibility thrown at me. How will I work? How will I function? I began experimenting with different forms of stretching. While lying down, my body would jerk and I would breathe weird.

One night, I felt as if someone hit me on the head with a pillow. I was terrified, believing there was certain to be someone else in the room, but there wasn't. That same morning my head raised up off the pillow, totally on its own. What followed this was a period where my body did involuntary movements and yoga moves. I knew nothing of yoga. I was a jogger for years and rarely stretched let alone twist my body into pretzel shapes. My limbs literally floated on their own. I was in awe.

I felt as if a force were taking me over. The energy worked out all my pain. I was elated off and on. I thought, "If the body is better. I'm better". There would be periods where the body would still and the mind would quiet at this time. Scientific formulas would come to mind and an understanding of how everything in the universe was connected. I would still have periods of weeping and going back to childhood memories. Something like a life review came up in my mind. I relived the horror of innocent and not so innocent wrongs I had done. I would have laughing fits. I would have a sense of no problems psychologically, as if all gates were open and plummet to horror and depression all in the same day. I began eating and sleeping

29

better after eight months of this intense phase. I began to work again. All the while the kundalini symptoms remained; the racing and intrusive thoughts. The elation, the involuntary movements, the anxiety and the spontaneous stilling of the mind, but I was in less pain and able to eat and sleep.

Recently, another phase of kundalini emerged. This time I experienced sinus drainage that initially tasted noxious and poisonous. I began seeing auras and colors. One night I sat wide-eyed watching a light show on my bedroom ceiling. With my eyes open, fully awake, I watched a huge blob of red move across the room. There were dots of purple, blue and many white lights raining down on me.

There were and still are lights in my head and I hear the sound of a flash on a camera going off. I began having dry heaves again and vomiting. My body would go into convulsions and it felt as if the me that I knew was being carried away. I've seen snakes and had several extremely vivid dreams. I hear buzzing like a swarm of bees in my head and feel pressure on my ears and sinuses. My ears pick up even the slightest sound and my nerves are extremely sensitive and jumpy. At times my body feels very small and at other times like a great giant. The ground wavers and quakes at times.

Meanwhile periods of stillness come over the body and mind. The body is totally receptive and alert. I see visions of rocks being pulled apart and light coming through. Sometimes it feels as if I'm jumping off these rocks. Other times I have visions of vessels emptying out, the bottoms pop off and water rushes through them.

Kundalini awakening is terrifying especially when one has no understanding of the process and is ungrounded. I have heard that some are trying to elicit this process through certain practices. This was startling to me when I first heard it. I feel spending one's time in this way is not wise and may even bring harmful consequences. The experience in full bloom can lead to delirium, insanity and even suicide. It is not something anyone experiences by choice and it is never what one thinks it is. Though the phenomena that emerges may appear spectacular to others, it is not something someone should seek for a thrill or even to become a better person. It does not make one a better person. When it emerges spontaneously without choice or seeking, it is enough just to get through one day and be present.

It continues to demand great awareness, questioning and an ability to let go. It is very easy to color the kundalini phenomena according to one's own desires and fears. This only keeps one stuck in it even longer. The kriya yoga is spontaneous. It is not meant to be elicited by practice and if it does come about by practice, it is not spontaneous. It is much better to work where one is at and allow one's own process to unfold. This is much more manageable psychologically.

In the midst of a kundalini awakening one is quite vulnerable and at times desperate. I was offered many different brands of antidepressants, muscle relaxers, pain medication and one doctor even wanted to give me something for Parkinsons. In my desperation, I tried some of these medications. Each one (with the exception of Paxil and Klonopin) accelerated the kundalini experience and increased my desperation. I also sought healers and movement therapists. The energy work and information regarding past lives, body trauma and psychological trauma that healers do increased all of my body sensations and ruminations. Movement therapy, though helpful partially to release stored memories, appeared to have no end. Each impulse and reaction brought another one and yet another. Where was the end I was searching for? These therapists were not able to answer my questions that burned in me as if my life depended on it. I remember saying in movement therapy, "I'm so stupid. I don't know I'm stupid. That's how stupid I am." This statement was serious to me, yet not understood and explored by my therapist. I also asked, "Can I relax when I'm afraid?" The answer I received was no, the body must act out fear. But wouldn't there be something else to act out then and then something else? And what are you when you stop acting? Are you finished then? If one is alive, one's body is always in action. None of this made sense to me.

I became very ill when I was doing Movement Therapy. A new phase of kundalini emerged and it debilitated me to the point where I wasn't able to work. I felt as if I was losing my mind and sat trembling in a chair for several days. I was fortunate enough to meet Ganga who explained that kundalini had completed for her. I remember several days sitting in front of the computer trembling reading her emails. She was able to answer all my questions clearly and give me advice on how to proceed. I was not looking for a teacher, but her support and knowing words have been the most important and helpful thing I've encountered. I was back to work and stable again after one month of knowing Ganga. I was anxious and confused about my experiences. I felt I was either chosen or possessed. I wasn't able to relax and kept myself on a psychological spin of fears. One feeding off the other.

She told me, "Don't color more into the experience than what it is". This made it easier to be with the experience and after it was over, simply drop it and move on. We talked about staying with the breath and not following the thoughts and drama in one's head. At times I have the understanding that the body is simply sitting, or walking and the drama in the mind just falls away and I realize the mind drama has nothing to do with now.

Also she's deep and yet light to be with. It's easy to laugh with her which helps to relieve the tension involved in not knowing what's going to happen next. We don't know what's going to happen, but Ganga says, "That's the fun part."

I feel a few people who tried to help me were sincere in their efforts. One can only give what one has and teach what one knows. I really needed and wanted someone who understood and didn't just give me sympathy and inadequate advice. I have been blessed to have met someone who followed kundalini through to the end and has come out on the other side. I consider Ganga my teacher and friend. The most striking statement she made to me was "Go through consciousness and the body will follow". When my body fell apart I was trying to do it the other way around. "If my body is better. I'm better." I'm certainly learning that we are much more than our body. My practice includes paying attention to the body and breath at all times. I do my best to not follow my thoughts and daydreams. When the silence comes, I'm just with that and don't make anything more out of it. When I'm walking, I just try to walk and that is all. This is the same with any other action. I question the self all the time, negate what is not the truth and try not to hold on to or second guess any results that might come. I try to witness myself in action, watch myself all the time and not rest too long in any one place psychologically. All of these things Ganga has helped to make clear for me. Kundalini is still with me all the time, but mostly I feel more relaxed about it. It's the hardest work of my life, but I don't know what our lives are worth if our suffering isn't for the good. If you are suffering with kundalini, I hope with all my heart that you will listen to the clear voice of reason and not get caught in the many pitfalls along the way. Keep going with it. Follow it through to the end. One last thing. Ganga knows what it is like to reach the end. She's able to answer questions because she has arrived there and is out of suffering. She explains clearly what enlightenment is and what it is not. This has also helped me to relax. Ganga is a living example that one can come out on the other side and be a true light to others.

Thank you Ganga.

Addition to first edition:

While Ganga was in India, the person I thought I knew began dissolving. I wrote a number of letters to her during this time asking for guidance and detailing my experiences. Those letters are included in this book and it is my sincere and honest hope that this writing will help others. I've come to understand that experience - no matter how spectacular or mesmerizing - is trivial and to deny it immediately. This helps clear the way for the new.

I want to say with all my heart that the no-self state is something attainable and realizable. It can happen to an ordinary person, living an ordinary life with the regular pressures of work, raising a family and the whole bit. For the self has entirely no support once questioned, pursued. The sincere longing of the soul to return to the source, in time and with persistence, easily overrides it.

Ganga's advice to shift from body identification to consciousness is key to this clearing process. Taking in the Gurus' words with total faith and quietude is essential. Believing that completion is absolutely real and possible must be part of the soul. Now, with or without the self, I wait in faith. I am so grateful that the right Guru came my way without effort on my part. I wasn't looking or shopping around. I will never do that. I feel it's a sad mistake and it encourages suffering and confusion. If you have found a sincere Guru, stay with him or her to the end. Shopping around is just to satisfy one's pleasures. All of which is very short lived. When one knows that only the truth will satisfy and is willing to risk all for it, then one is ready to really hear.

G: To follow is a very interesting and telling story about the kundalini and its sometimes great difficulties...I also suffered such heat and pain...and will give some words of encouragement at the end of your sharing...you are very close...you have touched the hem of the garment of truth...there is one more step to go...but first the sharing of your remarkable journey:

Burning Up, Fear, Dissolution. Pain of the World
L.L., Montreal, Canada

One Friday two years ago, I started having a splitting headache and lots of heat on top of the head. This I have known for years, and I used to control it by taking a cold shower or putting an ice pack. This time, the heat was so much I probably could have fried an egg there! In my room, the heat began to increase continuously, cold shower would not work. The whole night and the next day the body was just boiling inside, even a sip of water would increase the heat. I tried a cold bath and it got even worst. By the next day, Sunday by now, the inside of my whole body was just like an uncontrolled chain reaction and heat was still steadily increasing, I could not tolerate any clothing, and was on my knees crying on the bed.

I kind of knew what was going on having read Gopi Krishna's book *Kundalini* but really I was overwhelmed and there was nobody around to help, and how to help, what to do? From inside, I could see my skeleton white hot like an iron bar in a steel mill, the flesh inside felt like lava, all the body fluids seemed boiling, had no burns on the outer skin but even a bath towel dripping with cold water on my head would dry up in five to six minutes. My hands and feet were swollen and could hardly walk around in the room anymore to wet the towel. I was desperate. For a while I even thought that it was just my mind creating a demential illusion so I tried to accept and even love this heat, being grateful for burning my samskaras and whatever wrongs in the body. (This had worked well some years before when I was seeing all kinds of monsters and demons, loving them, accepting their apparition would just chase them away). But to no avail, the pain was too overwhelming.

Crying of pain, my mind began to be full of fear. The fear was not fear of death, I knew from many past experiences what death was (the tunnel, the light at the end and being turned back, so many times it had happened, was useless to want to die again). The fear was the fear of suffering more, of having more pain, I could not see how it could be possible. My blood felt like becoming more and more viscous and my heart just could not pump it anymore. Then the heart gave two mighty 'thump-thumps', two gigantic efforts and stopped. A moment later, all bodily sensations and awareness disappeared, I had jumped threshold of all the senses although I was still a witness inside, mainly from the back of the head. It seems that the brain continues to function for a while since I continued to be witnessing, I was not yet totally dead! One thought appeared in the mind and actually got inscribed on the screen of consciousness of the forehead, in big red capital letters: "SOMETHING STRANGE IS HAPPENING HERE" and then the inscription disappeared, floating far away, like one of these banners pulled by airplanes for advertising.

Words are kind of inadequate here but I was seeing my 'soul' beginning to disintegrate in small atoms and those atoms dissolving in a red and golden light and infinite void of consciousness. The sense of 'I-ness' was just being absorbed into this infinite field of nothingness; just then another thought came: "Hah, I am going home! Beautiful, great, finally!" By now the thinking process was kind of impossible, although thoughts would not form anymore, observation and memorization were still possible, it seems. And it was really beautiful, can't describe the witnessing of dissolving, dispersing and expanding more and more seemingly at the speed of light into an infinite space; colors started to change but memory is too thin here to describe, it was moving towards light-golden bluishness, maybe whitishness.

Then at some point, nearly when there was no more witnessing possible, it was like if all the dispersing atoms of my soul were being wrapped into a net as soft as a shawl of the purest transparent silk and slowly my 'soul' was put back together and pulled down back into my body through the head. Once there I started to feel the heat again. An immense disappointment began to dawn, I had been denied the 'going home' again! I began to descend slowly more into the body and at neck level I began to feel that the heat was coming down as I was gradually reintegrating the body. Few minutes later, I was aware enough to realize I was still naked on my knees on my bed, now shivering! I now could stand up although I had a splitting headache, it was now bearable and I could drink some water without raising the heat up and went into a deep sleep, exhausted after two and a half days and nights of suffering.

I had been 'dead' for maybe at least one hour or even more, can't be sure, from the time the heart had stopped.

It took a good six weeks before I had fully recuperated. In the meantime, I had had blood tests in order to find out if some bacteria or virus had not infected the blood and if this heat had not been caused by an inflammatory reaction of some sort but nothing was found. I had a couple of 'after burns' in the next two weeks which were kept under control with icepack on the head. Since then, the heat comes once in a while, especially when I am surrounded with chaos and loud agitation or eating food prepared by feverish people - it is a discomfort only. My neck is a major problem now, very often it gets shrunk down so much that the cervical vertebrae pop out of alignment. Yoga asanas help as well as with breathing while balancing the head back and forth.

Since, my psychology has changed a lot, kind of positively, more acceptance, more seeing that all that is around is an expression of some 'divine me'. When I notice negative things or situations with people, some emotions rise and bring sadness, I observe these things in wonderment and puzzlement, this can't be me, but still it is; not me directly per se, but as an other different expression of my being, kind of bizarre thing, especially in relation with things faraway like Afghanistan or what happens in Israel/Palestine and so on. Where my attention is emotionally drawn, I can't avoid seeing it as just another expression of some 'remote me'. I have to guard myself all the time not to get involved emotionally. Right now I am reading a book on the time of the partition in India, I cry almost every page, it is like being there, living these moments.

One month before September 11, I was crying every time during my morning meditation. When there were floods in Mozambique, I was hovering there, seeing people in trees, drowning etc. Same after the Gujarat earthquake for a while. I have become much more sensitive than I ever was and sometimes I only want to cut myself from knowing what is happening in the world or around me. Picking up feelings like that is irregular, and unpredictable, and do my best to avoid cultivating this, I can see that I could easily have an impossible life. But again, the worst feeling is having been denied this 'going home finally'. I feel my life being almost useless, terminated, nothing useful to do. What to do, maybe something will come soon but really I long for the 'trip home'. Wonder dear Ganga if you know a good travel agent, some Guru capable to provide a one-way ticket!

G: Yes indeed...what remains to totally surrender...when it comes again to let go...entirely and completely...into the hands of the Universal One... do not attempt to follow any thought or witnessing...let go completely...there is no need to not come back...if there is a total letting go of the self-identity with this then there will indeed be a new birth...and you will see that life is to be lived and enjoyed...Join the dance of Shiva...there is no separation of the One and the infinite transient play...but if it is let go of completely...then the Kundalini experience will indeed complete and end...Shakti will merge within Shiva...0 point balance will be entered into...No death remains for it is an illusion of body...as you have seen the self is made of energy particles pulled into an identifying pattern of unique expression... it is not separate from the One...so within the next round...when it begins, consciously let go...put the concepts and conditionings there on the altar of truth to be burned up as the dross that they are...do not fear coming back...it is a glorious Birth into the Eternal Self...

Energy Rushes and Anxiety. Guru and Balance.
Kali Anand, Tennessee

After my Kundalini Awakening, I was lucky enough to find Ganga Karmokar through an internet site called *kundalinisupport.com* created by Bob Boyd. She had done an interview with him that was not only strikingly moving in its own right, but immediately drew me in with connection to her. Unlike anything I had done before, I packed a bag before calling her and began the process of finding a flight from Nashville to Seattle that very day, unbeknownst to my husband.

Upon speaking with her, and communicating my experiences, she was ready with explanation and compassion. When I told her I needed immediate sanctuary, support, and counsel, she told me to come and that she would pick me up at the airport and pick up an extra bed on her way.

Of course, I'm getting way ahead of myself. My name is K****, and I am in the process of writing my doctoral dissertation in psychology. Up to my awakening, I was working at a university counseling center as a practicum student and a psychiatric hospital and finishing my graduate studies at Tennessee State University in Nashville.

I have been meditating since 1980, sometimes in the earlier years, hours at a time, looking to God for guidance and truth, and experiencing bliss and love for life and people. Even though, I had been experiencing a blissful energetic state since the 1980s, with experiences of heat up my back and orgasmic feelings in front that felt like blankets of the sweetest and most joyous love for God, gold light around my body and movements in my forehead and top of my head in meditation, I never really attributed any of this to a Kundalini awakening or rising. I have traveled extensively on service and spiritual trips such as to Nepal and Peru, always with God as a focus. Yet, I was the focus of the experiencing and sharing this love and bliss. It gave me extreme pleasure, energy, happiness and spiritual focus on others and of course, myself and on my own life.

In June 2002, my husband and I visited family in Texas, continuing on to Santa Fe, New Mexico for my husband's business concerns as a marketing consultant. On a stopover in Carlsbad, New Mexico, after reading my favorite verses from the *Tao Te Ching* of Lao Tzu, while my husband relaxed in the whirlpool at the hotel, we went to dinner. It was at this time during the meal that I began to feel stomach pains and went to the ladies room to actually lie on my stomach for a few minutes. The pain resolved, and once seated back at the table, I heard a roaring sound like the wind *whoosh* and the heat traveled immediately up my back and over my head. At this time, I recognized the sensation from previous experiences in meditation, but nothing as fast and as potent as this.

Initially, in Carlsbad, there were no immediate changes but once we arrived in Santa Fe, there were new events awaiting me at 7000 feet - and definitive changes. The next part of this continuing arduous journey had begun which I did not know then or even fathom.

The first night in the room in Santa Fe, again I experienced the heat up my spine, but this time with clamoring and energy rushes up and through my head, like electric circuits were firing up. I was left shivering beside my husband on the bed, as he lay sound asleep; luckily I was able to fall asleep that night. The next day my husband and I made our way around Santa Fe, but I began to experience unusual and short bouts of mild anxiousness and some other feeling possibly a slight dread? All of this would come and go and be quite mild. The second night I was unable to eat or sleep. Food was definitely not palpable to me, and the night brought with it another heated episode of discomfort and an aftermath of shivering. Needless to say, my husband was concerned, but couldn't figure out what was going on.

On our way back to Nashville I would experience minute feelings of anxiousness as if I had something immediate to be concerned with. We stayed at my family's house again for an overnight, and the night brought with it another difficult episode. I spent it alone lying on the living room floor. I was able to sleep in the early morning hours, and I was able to eat, but very lightly.

Upon returning to Nashville, I had nightly energy surges and no sleep for several days. Also, even though I was now eating, I was losing weight quickly. I finally told my husband I probably needed to go to the emergency room, but he couldn't figure out what we would tell them. So I decided to go to the doctor that same day with a book on Kundalini (I knew what was going on, but had no idea how to handle the immensity of the energy or any of the other symptoms taking place), and intuitively, I knew I needed guidance immediately!

The doctor took note of the book, stating he had heard of Kundalini, but that was as far as he went. He noted that I was hot, noted the weight loss, and lack of sleep so he suggested a thyroid panel (normal), and prescribed Ambien for sleep (which I used in 3mg, 5mg and 10mg increments and was a blessing, but now don't need). The best thing that came about from the appointment was the Ambien that gave me needed sleep over the following weeks because my mind felt like it was turned on twenty-four hours a day with vibrating energy. Meanwhile, I passed my orals for my doctorate and finished my last summer course; luckily the process seemed to give me respite on the occasions I needed it.

There were other kundalini symptoms such as: adrenaline rushes (some big, some small) as if my whole physical and mental self was in dire straits even though I might just be reading a book, and personal fears coming up right in my face that I had to look at. Also my head had tingling all over it, and my forehead felt heavy. These symptoms are still around in varying degrees, and although very uncomfortable to deal with at times, I have coping truths to work with now, and my bliss has made numerous returns usually when I think this is just too much. Coping truths are my name for the treasures I have received from Ganga, and continue to receive.

It seems strange, but in the initial stages I could not find solace in my spiritual practices, not wanting to even venture there, just holding on to God and my inner guru through the rough nights, but since then this has changed enormously. Through all this, I started to visit Bob Boyd's site regularly, hoping and praying that somewhere out there I could find someone for guidance. I emailed him some of my thoughts, and he responded, but it wasn't until I read Ganga's story and interview that I knew I had found my satguru. This is where I began my story.

Since being with Ganga, I have found myself in the presence of someone with great compassion, wisdom, strength, discernment and love. She gives without expectation, only to help others. She is an Enlightened one, not able to sit on the sidelines, but actively in center ring. One by one, she is willing to help others through this powerful awakening. She is tireless in her willpower in helping others through their unique journeys of life toward Self-Realization.

I have decided it is important to put down the insights she has given me, and although one must go through this process alone in terms of the awakening symptoms, one should not be alone without guidance or a teacher/guru. These are some of her words verbatim from me to you that have helped me unbelievably through this rite of sacred passage:

"When the fear comes up, don't label it fear or panic.
See it as simply a moving energy. Sit where you are and
do relaxed breathing, just watch it (Vipassana). Bring
yourself back to now. When the mind starts going, stop

and do something physical, or do mantra (OM). Do not chase after and cling to the mental stuff ever!!

You are working with consciousness, not body pathways. What you are looking at is mind-play that has created conditioning and your belief systems. Fears in the end are empty in nature. They will take you on a merry chase and keep you in bondage. Don't hang onto fears - drop them.

Source is not found within thinking; all action should be done in focused awareness of the moment. The awakening is not something you are battling, that is an absolutely wrong stance to take. When you battle back, you are feeding it. Fear feeds it. You are paying attention to it, and then emotions come into play. Breathing is used to relax. So go into the breath; it will give you a cushion, help you to look at it objectively. Once centered and able to witness it, you can confront conditions and fears as illusion and not solid. Go to the heart of it, and see that it is not valid!

If you are not on the path of ego, surrender and the universe will work with you. Fear arises when you are not surrendering the ego, when you are actively attempting to control. There is nothing to fear as everything comes from Source.

The illusion is that negativity has power, but it only has power because you give attention to it. NEGATIVITY IS IN FACT EMPTY. Everything in nature is empty; you must go beyond the intellect.

Surrender/acceptance and trust/faith rather than clinging, pushing, holding and grasping are imperative. Remember all you will feel and experience while going through your Awakening is transient, the roughest times and the most blissful! And remember true power is in loving and giving - Bhakti. Fear of completion/Self-Realization is a normal vacillation; eventually you will face the fear, and walk through it for liberation."

I will also add some of her email responses to me that have been invaluable to me back in Nashville:

K: *What do you do when the mind questions what to think as if it is emptying out and frightened of not having anything to think?*

G: Let it go! When thought ends there is just simply peace that remains! What is left is the unproductive mind drama…the ability to think is not lost…so simply let go…

K: *Is this because the slowdown of the mind? And does one just surrender to it?*

G: Yes - it is once again a justification of not letting go and surrendering to the process.

K: *The thing that is so very difficult is the transient changes in consciousness; there seems to be a consistent movement and change.*

G: This world is consistently transient and in flux. When entering the absolute then the stabilization will occur and remain. Source is unchanging within. That is your stability.

K: *I have identified some of the unpleasant aspects of the cleansing that continue in a circular fashion and change the energy flow. They seem to be universal fears/archetypal, and I ask how do I approach them in enquiry: as thoughts with no power, just go to the moment and breath, face them with enquiry alone to unmask them?*

G: Go to the heart of them - look at them square in the face and then dismantle it.

K: *Even though you know what is going on, you still have the tendency to feel anxiety, which I have stopped using as a label, and this change in energy is very hard to deal with. It is like being on a roller coaster with no idea where the next drop will be. I know you have spoken with me on this before, yet your communications are strong continual pillars and beacons through this: I am grateful.*

G: Once again go into the breath, use vipassana. See the energy change and let it release. See the mental dramas by stepping back and simply witness them. Don't get drawn into the drama of it. Then go into the core of it and dismantle through enquiry or Neti-Neti reasoning. Eventually it will be like a light switch being thrown. It will be dismantled and gone.

K: *I sometimes seem to be caught up in the awakening itself and not the goal of Realization of God, bliss and love and surrender. So I continue my practice toward this remembrance which brings bliss at times, and this will become all-encompassing, not an intellectualization but heart-centered.*

G: Don't focus on completion as it is already here, but only covered over...work on uncovering by seeing through the illusions playing out...stay heart centered. Keep working within the Bhakti of surrendering in love to the universe... Do OM THAT I AM Mantra.

Ganga enabled me to understand what was happening to me, and with just that, I was able to find some inkling of stability amidst my panic. She gave me breathing practice and walking meditation and just her presence and voice were stabilizing lights. She started me on a proper diet, and I began to gain weight, and started to be able to sleep. The most important thing was that I began to feel moments of bliss toward the ultimate sacred goal of Realization. Her Sunday Satsang gave me the opportunity of meeting others going through this, and to see her lovingly work with each unique individual on their path. Balance was possible, even through the roughest of experiences. I will be traveling with my teacher to India next month and feel grateful that I am able to do so. Thank you and love to you, my dear teacher!

Emotional Rollercoaster, Psychic Powers. Love.
E. B., Montreal, Canada

My life had always been emotionally difficult. I had been constantly subjected to high anxiety, severe depression and thoughts of suicide since my earliest memories. It seemed that nothing good ever came from my high moral standards yet I persisted in maintaining them. The more I loved and forgave, the more I felt hurt and taken advantage of. As a child, I was extremely religious and I experienced moments of blissful connection with God. In late adolescence and early adulthood, I began to meditate and do other spiritual practices and studies (Paganism, Kabbala, Rosicrucianism, Silva Mind Control). Siddhis came extremely easily which scared me as I feared becoming psychotic. I continued to meditate on and off throughout my life.

Nearly two years ago, I was once again contemplating suicide when I decided to once more try meditation and doing some yoga postures. I immediately felt positive emotional results so I continued to meditate and do postures. After a few months, I started to feel waves of joy go through my body. During the summer vacation, I went camping by myself and did a lot of EMDR (Eye Movement Desensitization and Reprocessing) by myself coupled with meditation when the process got too intense. The knot of anxiety I had always felt in my solar plexus changed and began to emanate pleasure.

Nine months into the meditation and yoga, I began to experience much synchronicity in my life and I became attracted to quartz crystals. I would become very high on happiness followed by bouts of depression which alternated quickly. I had trouble sleeping full nights and felt like I had drunk ten cups of espresso as my body was buzzing with energy. It was then that I met someone that told me that I was undergoing a Kundalini Awakening. I had no idea what that was...I was not religious, I did not feel comfortable using the word 'God'. I had always tried to live to a high moral standard and expect more of myself. I believed in love, compassion and forgiveness.

In my 10th month, I experienced what I was later told where the 'Gandhervas'. I am a high school teacher and while in class with my students, I fell into a state of rapture where I saw, experienced and heard through my heart these beings who were humming/vibrating joyfully and harmoniously.

In the 11th month, I was contacted by a spirit, whom I found out later is rather famous for having been channeled by others. He gave me information which I was able to verify on the internet but I told him to leave, not wanting to trust any spirits. He was not happy about leaving…

In the 12th month, while driving to school in a snowstorm, I suddenly realized/remembered that I had been a nun in Luxemburg. I saw her, I saw her convent, I heard her voice, I saw her bible, I knew her life. I felt such joy and love and saw my heart chakra expand as green energy six inches outside my chest. I felt such gratitude towards her as I knew that it was because of her and all that she had done that I had been born with such high morals.

In the 13th month, while meditating, I was brought out of my body, I expanded until the whole universe was inside my body, then I passed to another place that was all energy. I sat there a while, not understanding when I felt a presence behind me, enveloping me from behind and above my head. I asked this presence who it was and it answered: "Consciousness". This experience lasted a long time. Out of curiosity, I went to an internet site which gave far-sight tests. I was surprised to be able to view sites in my mind with amazing accuracy.

In all that time, I had no clear idea where kundalini was supposed to bring me. Thanks to Ganga, I learned about Duality and Non-Duality and finally understood what I should be focusing on, which practices I should be doing.

In my 17th month, after discovering Ganga on the internet, I put my awareness solely on my heart chakra as she suggests. I felt an intense love and yearning to be united with the Divine and I felt pulled into a white light while a powerful and exquisite feeling of love washed over me...

In the 18th month, I had an experience of "I AM" which changed me. I was no longer intensely aware of my chakras as I had been (only the heart chakra remained) and I lost the feeling of Love for the Divine. The feelings of bliss became more intense and more pervading throughout the whole day.

I still experience moments of sadness, mostly in the morning, just as I'm waking up. But even these moments are becoming less frequent and less intense. The rest of my day is lived in peace, calm and bliss of various degrees no matter what is going on around me.

My story is not a special one. I didn't have Kundalini rushes that made me gravely ill, nor anything of the sort that affected my health for the worst at any time. What I had, and am re-finding again, is the urge to know the Truth about what is happening with this body and mind that I used to call myself, about what is real and what is in my perspective of the world about what makes me, whatever this is, tic or tac about true Bliss and Freedom that I have always sought and never found. I found Ganga's site and started asking for her help on my path. From that point on, she has helped me beyond any help I would find possible for someone to give.

The four step process is really simple. The first step of the breath awareness as helped me balance out in ways I wouldn't find possible otherwise. It just works. After peace is attained the witnessing came quite natural to me. I haven't fulfilled the path yet, but I have no doubt, that the time is coming when I will release all and just enjoy this world for what it is myself.

Holy Frenzy, Savior Complex. Self Manifests.
An initiate

On the ninth night of an intensive vipassana retreat I came face to face with the fear of death. I felt utterly trapped - there was no way out. I could not cry, I wanted to scream and rip myself apart. I felt as if I would go mad. I stumbled behind the temple amongst the bushes. What followed was an experience that I described as 'something out of the bible'. I discovered that death is nothing to fear. My immediate response was, *dear God, no matter what happens, I am forever grateful.* I was changed overnight. I could not relate to what I saw in the mirror at all, but that did not matter. I had not realized I had been living in fear all my life and now I was free. I was literally glowing, my body felt like liquid slipping through liquid. I thought I was finished. It was actually just the beginning.

A couple of months later the kriyas began. Whenever meditating, my head would be yanked back and the upper back would automatically sieze up. The pain was great yet this force was pulling my head further and further back. At the next retreat I was told that I had active kundalini. I found Swami-G's website and sure enough, all the signs were there. Yet I was not interested in Realization - I decided that it all sounded so cold and harsh. I was a 'lover of God' - and what could be better! This 'holy frenzy' did serve the purpose of getting me through a lot of physical pain and illness. Yet something else was beginning to creep in...a deeper fear.

As this fear began to engulf the peace it was tough. I had always been able to do anything - achieve whatever I set my mind to - now just the thought of going to the bank would appear before me like a huge mountain to climb. I was walking about trying to relate to people when what was really going on, behind the scenes, was that I was poised on a tightrope between the earth and the sun and the whole universe was urging me to look at it.

Many synchronicities came forth, past lives emerged - things to let go of. Next there followed a period of spontaneous, constant prayer and contemplation of God. Then there was the pain of the world. Then the dark night of the soul. And still this fear, still tiptoeing along a tightrope. Out of this fear I began to personalize God. I began to have 'a relationship' with God, conversations with God. Insights came in a flash. Visions. Then there was another big shift into a state which Swami-G calls 'witnessing the witness'. Every object was buzzing with life, one big, surreal picture and 'I' was that which I looked at - an immense force, utterly pleased with its own creation. This was a helpful phase - there was no desire for powers as, who was there to impress when all was God? Yet still the savior complex had a hold - why would I be getting all these insights if I wasn't supposed to do something with them? *What about all the help I am being given? Shouldn't I be doing something in return?* I wanted to do the 'right' thing. Yet none of this made sense in the light of that which was seen in the 'witnessing the witness' awareness or the insights about mind and creation.

Finally I wrote to Swami-G because I did not want to get sucked into any more ego traps. I no longer wanted to be a 'lover of God' - even that 'me' could not be related to when I saw her in the mirror. The longing that had been steadily growing now intensified - whatever happened in this life, none of it was enough.

So all moves in its perfection...when that step needs to be taken, when everything needs to be let go of, then Self manifests. I arrived at the ashram and within two days there was a shift. This was entirely different from the 'witnessing the witness' state. Now the whole world was flowing from me on a gentle wave. Everything was glorious - not just the movement of the trees or the flight of a bird, but footsteps meeting the pavement or a truck driving blissfully past. Yet still it wasn't enough. There was still longing, uncertainty, fear. Two days before my time at the ashram was up, Grace emerged. A state of being which cannot be described. The kundalini process continues yet now the longing and fear has gone.

Kundalini Awakening in Both Partners
Anju

It has been almost one year since my kundalini awakening and I am still in complete wonder and awe about the experience, from the time it began to its continuing unfolding.

Never one to believe in religion, spirituality, the paranormal or even God, I had always prided myself on being a pragmatic and realist. Meditation, yoga and other new age activities were not things I really had taken an interest in or pursued. My then-boyfriend, Rich was the one who believed in ghosts and claimed unusual incidents happening to him throughout his whole life. I took a mild interest in this, but never took it seriously. When he began to do yoga spontaneously while asleep, then while conscious, I figured that was just something he did, as the odd one in my circle. Even when he began to speak in Sanskrit and make 'Om' sounds without knowing what he was saying or doing it purposefully, I shrugged it off as resulting from his difficult upbringing as a Jehovah's Witness.

I felt better about his new "talents" after he sought advice from a psychologist and from someone he called a 'Swami' up in North Seattle. He would talk about this thing called 'Kundalini' and frankly, I had no clue what he was talking about.

I'll have to admit that my awakening came the week after watching the film/documentary *What to the Bleep Do We Know*. It sounds silly, but I suppose it was the scientific, quantum theory discussions that led me to follow a piece of advice that one of the scientists said could help transform my thinking, and thus, my life. It was suggested that at night, before going to sleep, to think about a goal I really wanted to reach. Then, in the morning, before getting out of bed, I should ask God to show me that he is real, to show me with a physical, concrete sign. So I did. I ended up winning a prize in a drawing later that day, and I thought for sure that I had received some sign from above.

The next morning, I said the statement to myself again. I went to work, slammed the car door after arriving to the office and pulled a neck muscle. It hurt so much that I went home just an hour later to try to relax it. Rich, who was unemployed at the time was home. We took a nap together on the futon (which we have now decided carries special energy in it). I had fallen asleep - I think - or wasn't sure if I had at least, not fully.

Suddenly my body became electrified, like a lightning bolt had jolted all through my body, from the tips of my fingers to the end of my toes. Though the sun shined outside the window, everything went pitch black, and I could see lightning waves like you would across a TV or screen. I heard the sound of buzzing in my ears. It lasted for about thirty seconds, and was the most incredible, awesome feeling I had ever had.

I was never scared when it happened; I was actually quite thrilled that I might be going through kundalini awakening. I had Rich talk to Swamiji about it. Apparently, when one person experiences kundalini, they can trigger it in their partner as well. Swamiji told me that what I had felt was probably an awakening and I should come to Sunday meditation and Satsang. I did so happily, mostly because I wanted to experience that jolt of lightning again.

I closed my eyes during meditation, thinking that nothing would happen. By the end of the session, the area between my eyes had sort of squished together without any effort on my part. The next day, I meditated by myself after work. It didn't take long for the muscles to contract at the Third Eye again. This time, I saw blue/indigo lights. I was thrilled.

Things unfolded quickly for I went to bed that night, and as soon as I did, the Third Eye did its thing again. Though I thought all these experiences were cool, I started to worry that it was happening without my intending to bring it on. After a while, the muscle contractions moved to my lips. I began pursing them and moving my lips from side to side. I knew that what was happening was something huge.

Progressively, different parts of my body started to awaken. An hour or so had passed and I decided to wake up Rich, or perhaps my movements had woken him up. We both knew what was happening; kundalini was coming out with a force! It had become so late at night, Rich said to ask it to stop so that I (and he) could sleep. Somehow, it did stop enough for me to fall asleep. I thought it was over, but the muscle movements turned into mudras with an incredible, unstoppable energy. At times, I worried that the rapid circling of my arms and hands would lift me right off my feet. I cried spontaneously. It was a strange cry, for I was not sad, but my body was or at least, it wanted to release something.

Rich rushed me off to Swamiji who welcomed me into her apartment with open arms. My hands were flying faster than any conscious person could do. Swamiji balanced me with some energy work, and from time to time, my lips pursed so hard it looked like I was trying to kiss Swamiji. She took it light-heartedly.

Though I had clamed down for a bit after the energy work, I went home and had to keep going. Rich left me to attend a meeting. I sat by his alter and stretched myself in numerous yoga positions, though I had never learned yoga. By this time, my body was so sore. But I continued, I had no choice.

Rich came home and for some reason, my body was just drawn to his. I started doing energy work on him, without knowing what I was doing, just letting it happen. He had told Swamiji that since I started awakening, he felt very funny inside. He laid down on the magical futon, and I put my hands on his stomach. After a few strange sounds coming out of my mouth, my voice began to say, "I will help you." I was overcome by the words. Our souls were talking to each other.

My energy brought out some pent-up feelings that Rich had been holding onto. He revealed some things in his past that he wasn't proud about; I did the same. Many other amazing and incredible things happened that night. We got hints into what had been driving some of Rich's problems, and mine.

I realized that all of us, whether we are conscious of it or not, carry with us deep-seated experiences either from this life or past lives that affect what we do. Through kundalini this karma be changed.

That night, I had what Swamiji called a lower samadhi state: God Realization. Though I thought my relationship was over with Rich, I had never been so happy to know God existed and that I would never be alone again knowing that God was with me.

Had it not been for the sanity of Swamiji, Rich and I would not be together today. By this time, after what I had been through in those two days, I had nothing but the utmost respect for Swamiji (or Guru-ji), her divinity and her path in life. I took Diksha the next day, and then I became initiated as Anju; one who lives through the heart.

Rich and I ended up getting married, with Guru-ji as our officiant. There have been many incredible, brilliant and yes, scary experiences with this kundalini journey, practically on a daily basis. Sometimes Rich and I go through things together, sometimes separately. But with the stripping down of each layer, I feel closer to my true self, my inner being, my purpose in this life. My Diksha name has become a guide to what I need to do to progress on this path. I am always grateful that my journey has been made easier with Rich trailblazing the way first, and of course, with Guru-ji as my teacher.

If there are any doubts about the power of kundalini or about the grace of guru-ji, please take this testimonial into consideration. The journey is scary and difficult without someone like Guru-ji to guide you through this path.

Thank you Guru-ji for all you have given to me and to so many others.

PART 4

Guidance

KUNDALINI
Phenomena/Symptoms

- The Blue Light
- Seeing of auras
- Heat up the spine (can be extreme)
- Cold feeling flooding a chakra area
- Feeling the Nervous System is short-circuiting (can be extreme)
- Pulsing energy at the base of the spine (can be painful)
- Red flame pattern over heart chakra area
- Sounds heard internally:
  o Birds
  o Trains
  o Bells
  o A hissing or whistling sound
  o Someone quickly saying something (like "Ha!")
- Extreme sensitivity to sound, vibration etc...
- Siddhis ('powers') such as complete knowledge of something
- Feeling what is happening in someone else's body
- Picking up the emotions of others
- Normal photographs that pick up light phenomenon, mists etc.
- Body awareness changes: feeling larger/feeling smaller
- Feeling as if you are 'here and not here'
- An absolute absence of thought
- Bliss
- Extreme Fear (note: this one is temporary)
- Dreams of snakes and fires
- Dreams of religious and spiritual symbolism
- Samadhi states of feeling utterly connected with ALL - yet also witnessing and not involved...
- Finding the consciousness expanding to where you are not in the body (eg: seeing over the trees while you are at ground level)
- Spontaneous mudras (hand gestures)

- Spontaneous asanas (body postures)
- Body may move with certain music - uncontrolled pulsing or swaying
- Feeling as if you are in a strong earthquake
- Ability to manifest what is needed - once again, a siddhi but do not attach to these phenomena, let them go...
- Seeing of internal lights (flashing lights in vision/rotating light)
- Seeing the world in enhanced coloration
- Yawning - Laughing - Crying

This is a partial list - no two people have the same manifestations.

KUNDALINI
How Does It Get Started?

Kundalini may become activated by many ways. Here is a short list:

1. By direct Shaktipat (like one battery charging another).

2. By prayer and sincere seeking the truth and dedication to serving mankind.

3. Through an intense shock to the system.

4. Through childbirth.

5. Spontaneously - due to past lives working in this area.

6. Through Reiki - either having done, or working with.

7. By participating in any Chi-oriented martial arts system.

8. Through yogic techniques.

9. By drug use.

10. From Trance activities with heavy pranic overtones.

11. By pranayam (breathing exercises)

12. Through re-birthing shocks

The ways and means are expanding and it is becoming more and more common to see kundalini awakenings come to the forefront. Now, once begun some will have a short blast - a one experience - and then recede, but many will indeed, once started continue on until one completes the journey by blowing out all held conditionings and egoistic self ideas that wrap around form and body mind images.

What Is The Purpose Of Kundalini?

Kundalini is a concentrated moving energy, it moves through the mental, emotional, physical and causal bodies. This energy or moving conscious awareness travels through the body systems and activates all the cellular memories - all the conscious and unconscious held knowledge and beliefs. Once begun, it travels through the bodily system and the seven layers of Conscious Awareness, bringing to Consciousness directly through symbolism, feeling and thoughts, everything that has been perceived, stuffed, held, or believed for review and discrimination.

It is a process of being able to see all the causal avenues and to clear them, once more going back to what is termed Original Mind or Clarity or Self-Realization or the Enlightened State of Being. In seeing and confronting directly the causal conditionings that create ego identity and bondage they lose their hold and are transcended. Within the last step of being drawn into Source or Nirvikalpa Samadhi they are in essence shattered and no longer valid to your experience. This is why there is so much bodily activity and pain due to the opening of cellular memory. It of course will pass as do all things. But what is important is not to focus on attempting to move more energy from blockages but to relax and be able to diffuse it by understanding it. Then the blockages are opened and transcended.

Once kundalini is activated what is needed is to relax and learn to walk the middle path of balance. The Kundalini will move of its own accord. Your mission is to simply see what is rising and to continue to diffuse it by understanding and by surrender.

Kundalini is not positive or negative within itself, it is Neutral or Satvik in nature. It is your attention that perceives it as positive or negative.

Once again: Kundalini is a process of bringing up all the cellular memories of self and the evolutionary mind of mankind to be dealt with and walked through. It takes you through the seven levels - realms - or layers of consciousness to walk through every paranoia, fear, illusion, play, egoic ideation, conditioned response, and concept that you have ever held or encountered. Once begun it cannot be closed. This is why it is imperative to have a kundalini completed teacher that accepts the responsibility of helping you to completion. This is why the devotee/guru relationship is indispensable. The Guru not only guides the Sadhaka but by their presence, but also helps to balance and also accelerate their growth. This has inspired this book - because there are so many that are lost within the midst of kundalini awakenings. To wander through it alone can be truly attempting to navigate a hell realm and maze that can keep circling endlessly. What I offer is a way through the maze and realms to liberation instead of madness.

Seven Realms or Layers of Consciousness

Within some Buddhist studies the layers of Consciousness are called realms. Within Hindu texts they are called chakras. The realms or layers of Consciousness hold personal and also mass mind awareness or planetary consciousness as well. What you are traversing is the planetary karmic path and evolutionary mind as well as your own identification within it. We will go through each of the layers.

In each of the layers you will more than likely process through your positive ideations and feelings within it as well as the darkened ideations or colorizations of a negative nature. Remember this that in the end ALL comes from the Source. The positives and negatives are created and sustained by mind/body/emotional attachments to persona. Once you have broken through the persona attachment then the conditionings attached will also shatter and be cleared.

As the kundalini process continues, each layer of consciousness encountered will bring forth feelings, symbolism, dreams and direct cognitive experiences through form and within thought to be seen and confronted. Eventually it will reach a point in which one must see through the illusion of it and dispel it by surrender 100% to Source within.

Number 1 Mind Set or Realm to transit is that of Survival

The first level you will transit is that of survival maintaining your life. This brings up all the fears that are concerned with enough money, food, shelter, and keeping yourself safe...This will bring forward the 'fight or flight' response. You may become concerned with self-survival, also with planetary survival. Be aware what may arise are fears and phobias concerning personal safety and also the fear of death. Here is where there is a great emphasis given to taking supplements and exercising - all things that attempt to prolong life. While it is wise to take care of the temple, there needs to be balance in all things. This is the number one basic realm.

A balance in this area is one that sees the continuity of life. Sees the patterns of change and accepts that death is not the end but simply a moving onwards to a new experience... Life is no longer feared but entered into fully.

Number 2 Mind Set or Realm to transit is that of Sexuality

The second level is closely integrated with the first; that of sexuality. There could be either over-abundance wherein the sexual energies feel out of control and are indulged in excessively or it may also go the other way where they may be turned down or denied. This is a big trap for many. This is why many gravitate towards the practices being touted as 'Tantric'. This type of Tantric exercise is a two-edged sword for it most often is entered into by those seeking a way to use the sexual energies to progress.

Tantra is not about sexuality and therefore those chasing after this medium will encounter only more bondage. Many think that this sexual energy must become balanced - male/female. That again is a misperception. What needs to be balanced is the outflow. Sexuality is neither to be repressed nor chased after. Once kundalini begins, balance in all things is required. Repressed sexuality only leads to a mind that runs away in unhealthy avenues. The way to Self-Realization is not through sexual avenues. Only one whose focus is totally away from self and 100% surrendered within the Divine may use this path as a way to liberation. Otherwise it may become simply another trap of Maya and egoic pleasures in the name of spirituality.

Keep your sexuality in balance. Honor your partner. Don't use it for selfish means. Don't fear it. Don't negate it. Don't chase after it. Keep it as a part of nature and in balance. Some caught in this realm try to exude sexual appeal and see conquest or clinging as part of their identity. Procreation and having children is a way that some feel able to ensure their ongoing identity.

A balance here is what is needed regardless of whether one may or may not be in a relationship - but a healthy wholeness may be fully shared within a relationship. A healthy relationship sees and shares on all levels of intimacy.

Number 3 Mind Set or Realm to transit is that of Personal Power

The third level you will transit is that of forming your personal identity and creating success - becoming either a mover and a shaker or feeling like a failure. Worrying about the success of yourself, company, country or world. This is the one where status comes into play and also, competitiveness. The personal sense creates the need for either status or recognition in competition. This is where the push occurs to have more, be more. There is either; being an authority; or fearing authority, on the negative end. This will either push to establish or tear down. This is the realm of military might and moguls. This is a big egoic realm. A difficult one to traverse.

Within this realm comes critical evaluation of yourself and others. Attempting to come up to a certain level of 'success'. Those that are not within the push mode are in the ideation of being put down, depressed, have issues with authority, some will do anything to avoid any level of confrontation.

The balance here is where success is not seen as an outside accomplishment but as simply being who and what you are without any need for external kudos or displays. There is no need to 'become' anything as everyone is at core level the same essence and valuation. None are higher or lower.

Number 4 Mind Set or Realm to transit is that of Heart Awareness

In this level come the ones whom are either out for themselves or on the other end of the spectrum, those that are the "humble servants of humanity". Those that have no heart opening are only wrapped up within their own identification and self-serving motions and motives. There is no compassion for others nor thought about anyone's welfare except their own. These are those that prey upon society to fill a hole that will not be filled.

Then there are the 'do-gooders' that perform all the right outer actions but are doing it for self-recognition. These are the humble martyr types dripping with humility and good works. Unfortunately the motive is; *just look at how humble I am.* Many want to save the world even though they cannot save themselves and live in misery. This is a huge hurdle within the spiritual path. Some attempt to help others as a way to fill the hole or gap of pain that they themselves live within. Some confuse Agape Love with sexuality and wind up attempting to live within two realms at once. Some think that 'love' means saving the world - whether the world wants it or not.

A balance in this area consists of resting within a total wholeness and contentedness within yourself and all life. Moving in a spontaneous motion, compassion and empathy will occur as needed. Agape Love is not grasping but a contented Knowing that ALL are simply the One. Love is a sharing of who you are, what you are and giving what is needed in an appropriate way without looking for rewards.

Number 5 Mind Set or Realm to transit is that of Creative Endeavor - Vibrations

This is the land of the dark void, bliss or poison. This is where words may come through and the insights of various texts may become clear. Here is where you create by voice patterns of energy. All creation is simply energy moved by mind and conceptualization. Here is where you live and speak your truth or error...here you actively enter creation...*In the beginning the word was with God and the word was God*...Word makes creationary drama. As you change your focus your language will also change. You are what you speak.

All of creation comes from vibration patterns. This is the realm wherein you focus on the positive or negative and project it by the spoken word. Here the words and wisdoms may come as concepts and glimmers but do not think that they are what you are seeking. There is still further to go...So do not turn away from enquiry and mindfulness yet...There is yet further to go on the path...Here is the danger of equating knowing about with Knowing...OM - the highest mantra that takes one from division to one pointed focus...OM takes one from sound to silence. OM takes one to the subtle formless...

A balance in this area is one wherein balance is entered where one no longer chases positives or negatives. Where spontaneous words of compassion and wisdom flow.

Number 6 Mind Set or Realm to transit is that of Mental and Subtle Realms

In this realm one enters into subtle phenomena; lights, astral planes, siddhis - this is the land of the last crossing...Mara or 'intellectual delusion' plays very subtle tricks to keep the ego in play...here ego can be seen through...Here is where the siddhis must be let go of...Here is where the mind either goes off on subtle experience or surrenders to the silence and One. All phenomena is of the realm of creation. To reach beyond creation and creator to Source this realm must be passed through...

Here is the last great barrier...Here it is that you must be diligent and not be pulled into the world of psychic and paranormal...Here is where you must be firm in your commitment to turn your back on siddhis and powers. Here is the place where surrender is paramount...Where Neti-Neti (or 'not this') should be used when phenomenon start to pull you in...It is here that you can start to lose the self-identity and can begin to enter into a Sarvikalpa Samadhi...

When balanced, the intellectual mindplay ends and stilled awareness prevails...What is required comes as required - nothing need be held. Sarvikalpa Samadhi is found here...

Number 7 Realm is entered here...Beyond the Mind

Here in this realm one enters into Non-Duality. One passes through the demise of the false egoic mind and conditionings. Blown out and shattered, what remains is the Non-Dual Reality.

Here is where one goes beyond mind and the senses into a Nirvikalpa Samadhi...Into the Primal Source or Essence...the Pregnant Void of Infinite Unending Potential...Place of THAT which is beyond birth and death...within Here all is stripped bare then spit back into life as a new creation...From here One will descend back into either heart or wisdom... there will be spontaneous action which has no center. This is the end of the search but merely the beginning of Life.

Balance is when Sahaja Samadhi remains. Where Advaita/Dvaita are ever Non-Dual in nature...for within integration within Nirvikalpa Sahaja Samadhi the world of phenomena and transient are known to be empty in nature...Liberation remains if conditionings and egoic mind are not pulled back in...

Questions And Answers

1.   What does the Kundalini do?

Kundalini is an energy force...Concentrated Consciousness that moves when awakened through the three bodies (physical, subtle, causal)...Moving through the physical body it releases all past and present vasannas and samskaras, to see and go through...until they are dropped and cleared...

Although having a great impact on the physical form it, in the end, has little to do with form at all...but simply to go beyond ego to merge with the Formless Constant or Pure Conscious Awareness, the Emptiness of Being which all form merges from and returns to...During its upwards journey the three bodies are traversed...Or you may say the physical, mental, and emotional bodies will be cleared...On this journey you will see and experience many levels but remember all are only mindplay, movements of consciousness...the power and energy comes to a halt when the kundalini experience reaches its end destination which is loss of ego and merging with the Source...within the Source there is only clear light, the power ends as there is no longer any movement...From there you will once again enter the flow of life - Being simply Truth, Consciousness and Bliss...clear of all past preconceived notions and illusions created by the forms experience...There is no longer a feeling of "I am this form" but rather, the Universe is Consciousness Moving...There is no "I" separate from Consciousness... Only Consciousness beyond the form remains...Ever conscious of the One and knowing the many to be only seeming aspects of the One...

2.   On entities and fears during the kundalini experience:

Take this for what it is worth - it is from my own personal experience...During the kundalini process, for a couple of months I lived in absolute fear and terror...This thing would come...like an evil energy that would be so close as to almost surround me...and I would be in terror...at one point I was

66

literally on the floor, crouched in a fetal position with my hands covering my head...I am surprised that my hair didn't turn white overnight due to the terror...there was at the same time an irrational fear that if I touched my daughter she may become possessed...

What I found was that in fighting this thing, the intensity only grew...what worked in the end was in absolute surrendering to God and just sitting through it...seeing it without reaction...it is all only an illusion of the mind...but make no mistake it feels absolutely real and concrete at the time...but it is ALL the fears and conditionings coming to a head...and manifesting in your face literally...It will dissipate as the illusion that it is when you can just sit through the experience without giving it any energy...it is all only a play of mind...and we must walk through our 'terrors' to see that they are only illusions...so have no fear...just face it head on...and give it no energy...just submit ALL to God and then let it come...and it Will dissipate...your fear fuels the fire...You will make it through...just let go of the fear and trust God within and the illusion will shatter...

3.   What about siddhis?

Siddhis come and go...in attempting to hold onto any of them you get caught up into more ego...to the point of egotistical belief that you are a superior creation far above the masses...this is a dangerous and quite real trap...Those not ready fall into it quite easily... and in their self-importance they fall ever farther away from truth... Just because siddhis manifest it does not mean that you are spiritual...if you are sincere in wanting to reach Realization you see the trap and do not use the siddhis...let them fall away... they are nothing in the end...what is there to control...only ego...only the egotistical want to control...so if someone is boasting about their powers and siddhis RUN, do not walk RUN in the other direction...for this one is lost in a delusion of his own creation...Maya sets many traps along the way...those that are not purifying their thoughts, not coming from the heart, not surrendering to the Source will definitely get caught in these traps. ENERGY may be used or MISUSED...it is directed by Consciousness... if mind gets into the play it can be misdirected...

4. Q: I would very much appreciate any insight you may have on the subject of uncomfortable and not so happy inner experiences.

G: These things arise through symbolism...do not take it to be literal happenings...this is all the repressed stuff shoved together in one big mix...and it comes forth in a number of ways...but do not cling to any of these manifestations...they are simply repressed mind images and emotions and conditionings surfacing...(sure, easy for me to say)...but I tell you that you can and will make it through...if you 'know' that they have no substance... simply the same substance as a dream state...so have no fear...it is only when you cling to them that they will appear to have concrete form...

5. Q: Do experiences that are kundalini-related result in:
    a) paranoia of varying degrees?

Yes it can...depending on how much you attach to the experiences at hand...if a lot of fear is rising and the manifesting occurrences take on a sinister appearance...it is quite possible to go into a type of paranoia...but once you can see beyond the happenings and know that they are simply mind-generated illusions you can move through it...when you can come to the point of surrender and not give any energy to these type of happenings you will balance out and the manifestations causing the paranoia will end immediately...

    b) lightly to heavily disordered thinking?   (Missing references, tautological reasoning that is circular, a sense that we don't have to provide 'evidence' of our assumptions or conclusions.)

G: The thinking processes are altered along the way...you go from relative and logical thought that is built upon one experience to another within form...to where the mind stills and the relative thought processes stop...and within that transition various and manifold changes occur. There can occur, during the process, heavily disordered thinking - depending on how you are reacting to and interacting within the process...as the mind is slowing and you are entering into a higher awareness - you can go through a period where you appear to space out - you can miss whole passages of what was said just the moment before...this will adjust later down the road...sometimes you go directly to an end and there are no logical steps to that end...information and knowledge on certain things just appear within the framework of consciousness...it does not mean that the end conclusion or awareness is wrong...there is NO evidence for some experiences...you cannot 'prove' by evidence the experience of Nirvikalpa Samadhi for it is beyond the five senses and thought...you can only 'prove' what is seen and known in the relative world experience...what is beyond that cannot be 'proved' except that it is a singular experience...within Realization or Nirvikalpa Samadhi there is only ONE experience and Truth that is known...which shatters all the formerly held beliefs...what emerges is a singularly held Truth…in this you can know that it is a true experience…in that what you know to be Truth is supported by the great scriptures and the sages throughout history...it is not something that has been studied and memorized and intellectually known - it is 'KNOWN' 100% by direct experience... and that experience is unshakable...

c) generalizations? - I'm right on the borderline with this one: implicit sense that kundalini experiences are 'special' and that everyone is not experiencing them in one form or the other. (Could it be that that kundalini is almost synonymous with adaptive dysfunctional response to experiences within a certain spectrum of normal human capacity?)

G: There are those that will create within their minds, with great imagination, a false kundalini experience...not everyone is experiencing a kundalini experience...and not everyone is imagining a kundalini experience...kundalini is simply an unfolding of consciousness...an energy which directs the consciousness to move through all the preconceived notions and self-created bondages created and held in place by our own belief system and thought...Special? What is special? Just as in Realization there is nothing special in it; in that ALL will come to eventually know the truth of Who and What they are and are not...what is special about that?…and yet it is simply also a fact that there are precious few who truly 'know' beyond a shadow of a doubt what is God...and what is existence...and just where they fit in the scheme of things...or who achieve that inner peace which comes from that direct experience...but it is the Essence of simply unfolding Life...and what is beyond this limited life experience...

6.   Can you please tell me if only a truly enlightened person/God-realized person can give Shaktipat, or is Shaktipat a yogic power - that one who is not totally enlightened, can acquire?

G: Shaktipat is a yogic power...it does not mean that the one that possesses it is enlightened. Many give shaktipat as a matter of course...not taking into accountability where the person receiving is at - mentally, emotionally or spiritually...many are facing many problems and a difficult path due to an awakening by a well-meaning but unqualified guru... I am sure that these gurus are not meaning to hurt anyone...but in fact, it happens...when the kundalini is going strong it is possible to give shaktipat to another... Just as when one battery is well charged you can charge and jump start a dead battery...it does not mean that the charged battery has any greater intelligence than the dead battery...it is simply an energy...but if it is directed by humble intent and a desire to know truth it will be constructive...It will burn away the dross one way or another in the end...Please do not make the mistake of thinking that just because someone has a lot of kundalini activity and energy that they are necessarily enlightened...

7.   What about kundalini and sexual feelings for the Guru who has given us our start with kundalini?

G: Once again I can only speak from what has happened within my own realm of experience...but yes, there are those that are misguided that think that sex is a way to balance their energy...and of course, the guru or anyone with an apparently awakened kundalini is up for grabs, so to speak...many things happen that we do not consciously control...much to the mis-belief of those that we work with - such as appearing to them in dreams or in visions, etc...and things get transferred to the guru or teacher...the newly awakened feelings of bliss or compassion sometimes can be misconstrued as love for the teacher...and the teacher's compassion can be taken as a come-on...sometimes this has happened...in those cases I have had to let the student be on their own until that ideation was corrected...there are those that take and cling to the teacher or guru in an inappropriate manner. They wish to be as close as possible - and in a misidentification between Agape Love of the teacher (which is extended as a matter of course) - they, in their illusions, twist it to a sexual ideation...or also as an over-clinging 'neediness' for the guru...this is why some choose not to have an ashram...just to divert some of this that naturally arises due to the aspirants' changing perceptions being clouded by previous conditionings still held...this is why it is impossible to let students get too close on an ongoing basis...at least this has been my experience to date...

8.   Did the Self-Enquiry eventually smooth out and complete your kundalini process?

G: YES!!! Without this very, very important avenue this one would surely still be within the throes of the kundalini experience...for all experiences within kundalini stem from the mind and consciousness to bring you to the point of seeing the illusion of ego self and Maya...it is the long route to go through the siddhis until you find out that they do not bring wisdom nor peace...simply subtle experience...experience within the subtle planes...but all the subtle planes still lie within the realm of mind...Within the Self-Enquiry process the ego self is peeled away...you see and come to Know...not as an intellectual concept (which may be grand for a moment but does not bring lasting change...) that you are Not the mind, nor body, nor emotions etc...When you break through that into direct knowing, the conditionings that have kept you bound will just dissipate immediately...but there is still a ways to go...from there you go beyond body consciousness and into utter surrender...and finally to the door of the great unknown and unknowable...and in crossing that last barrier within the shattering of the ego ideation - the last vestiges of concepts, etc. implodes...and the kundalini ends...you reach to the Heart of Being...and when the kundalini reaches into the heart after traversing up to the Seventh Chakra then the journey is complete...Consciousness has reached beyond mind and conditionings to pure Awareness...or Source or the Heart of Being...From then you will once again come back into body awareness but from that moment on the conditionings do not return...resting ever within the Stability of the Constant, the transient realms of Maya are traversed as the great miracle of the non-dual...for confirmation of what is being said here you may want to read that which Sri Ramana Maharishi has said on this very subject...you will find that it tallies with this writing...

9.   Is this "Dark night of the soul" an essential state for every individual seeking Realization?

G: Although it is not essential as anything is possible... it is for the most part a valid happening for most on the path...do not attempt to bring up such an occurrence...if it happens it is arising to draw you to center...if you are already moving towards center then perhaps it may be bypassed...

10.   Since the time comes for you to "confront all your fears and weaknesses" - could you please tell me what happens if you fail in the test for one of those weaknesses?

G: If something is not passed through then it will re-manifest in some other avenue until it is successfully seen as illusion and walked through...all attachments will continue to manifest on some level until they can be successfully let go of...but yes, the last point to walk through is usually the great fear of self-individualized loss...the ego death...the last precipice of the unknown...

11.   In many places, you have mentioned that ego death is a fearful stage. Is it still fearful if you are ready to sacrifice your individuality for Realization? If that is not the point, could you kindly explain why is this a difficult phase.

G: it is one thing to intellectually realize that the individual ego must be at an end - must be sacrificed to Truth...it is quite another when that reality is about to take place...it is stepping off into the void...the unknown...You will know this eventuality only when you are at that last veil of separation...if you have total faith within your Self and your Guru your transition may go smoother...

12.   What about kundalini and celibacy?

G: While suppression is not always the answer, neither is wanton sex...Brahmacharya is a state of mind...To be pure and chaste within...To not cling - to be within emptiness - a gentle silence...When the Bliss within is found and uncovered then it will radiate...When wholeness within is found and rested in then the need for an outward coming together is no longer chased after...The wholeness being sought is always in the end found within the Heart of your own Being...

13.   I think the one question that haunted me for the longest time was: what were the visions and voices all about? Where did they come from and why did they suddenly stop? It was the most difficult part of the process. I found myself stuck, desperately wanting answers and I still don't have a grasp of what happened and still feel a little fearful of meditation in case it all stirs up again.

G: All that comes up is from your fears, trepidations, cellular memory, reason and symbolism to look at all your conditionings. What may also come up are indeed from the mass mind memory. But Always be cognizant that it is ONLY a thought or voice or vision and can in NO WAY harm you...There is no reason to fear anything that comes up...Simply go into the breath. See it and when distanced enough from it, Go into it deeply to see what the source of it is...Once seen the illusion surrounding it will be known. Then it will simply be gone...Don't fear your meditation, stay centered and use the methods in the 'Tools' section to progress...

14.   Is it necessary to have the 'Kundalini experience' in order to attain Self-Realization?

G: No not per say...but each that are on a spiritual path have some type of conscious energy urging them onwards...

15. Should the kundalini experience be sought out? Should one try to get it activated?

G: No...In processing kundalini one should be under the guidance and care of a kundalini completed guide and Guru...One that is completed can help to balance and also accelerate the process if time is spent in their presence...But all that is needed is Self-Enquiry. Kundalini awakening just puts everything in your face where it has to be addressed...

16. If not, how then should one proceed without having the kundalini in process?

G: Through Self-Enquiry and simplifying the life, taking the road of mindfulness…a Zen approach...

17. Can you say something about the fear of losing the sense of self.

This is the last barrier that is faced...the last great fear to be transcended, that feeling of utter extinction that happens when you reach the veil between 'knowing' and entering into 'unknowing' or 'Self' minus the ego ideation of body, mind etc...While it is true that you know that something will not survive...and this is not unfounded...for in Truth there is no 'thing' to survive...the thing was simply the ever moving mind of concepts and the body of illusory experience...these are shattered in that instant of utter release... and what remains and what has always been is absolute Abstract Intelligence... Peace...Bliss...Awareness minus the judgments and singular distinctions...Life is known as it has always been simply extending from that Eternal Purity of Consciousness which moves and creates Energy and Form in patterns which is called Existence and Creation...and the 'Self' minus identification resides within and through ALL of existence... and yet is separate as it is ever unmoved or touched by any of the happenings within the created realm...

It is great freedom when the ego identification has ended...when you are not...when you are not then you are also ALL...yet moving within the Pregnant Void there is simply a seeing manifestation as it rises from that silence and void into seeming patterns which rise and fall due to the conscious movement which is created by the mass mind...the grand illusive play called Maya...but being at that point beyond the illusions you see it as just the ever expanding dream called 'life'...there is no longer death nor life...for you have ever been that which is beyond both these seeming aspects...when the last barrier is traversed then the ideation of life and death recede...into the oblivion of illusion that was created by the identification with body and form...You are ever free...Being and Non-Being...Beyond both...Totally the ever present Paradox...and it matters not whether seeming in form or beyond form - for form is simply an identification with mind, body, and divisionary concept...Therefore for that One that has transcended form it is no longer a binding image...others see it but for you it is as the finger is an appendage of the hand...the hand is not aware of the finger - it simply is...and so you move through existence...seeming to be in form...yet unconnected to it...not bound by its seeming parameters...

To transcend the last barrier takes letting go...submitting all to the universe...to the Self within...while 'Self' is a misnomer for there is no feeling of personality attached to it...yet it is the Foundation or the Source which makes all experience possible...therefore at core it is termed 'the Self'...it is more apt to say the great 0...for that is all that remains...The Emptiness which contains ALL of life...For life is ever the Great Eternal Moment ever-changing patterns called 'mind' and the unchanging Constant called God or Source or Consciousness Itself...That - beyond questions and answers is the Great Peace and Bliss...It simply remains aware of the great show...and is at rest within the space of Expansion where within and without no longer carry meaning for they are of mind and Maya's play...You are ever the play and the player and yet are unconcerned with either...Once again the Paradox which IS...There is simply that ISNESS that remains...seeing yet not seeing...Hearing yet not hearing...Being yet not Being...ONE yet 0...in eternal harmony...Have faith and release the hold of ego self and the last barrier will be slipped beyond...the last illusions will shatter...and what remains is what has always been the Constant beyond the illusive ideation of the transient...

18.   Kali and Kundalini

G: Kali is very interesting...Kali proceeded from Durga to fight the last and most powerful of Demons...and just what was this Demon that was being fought? Ego...hahahaha...so you see it is ego and mind which bring the delusion of Maya and keep one seemingly bound in Karma...and it is within the destruction or implosion of ego that liberation is won...therefore Kali is seen wearing the skulls and limbs of mind and body...and chopping off the head of ego...she wears the skulls; the number being that of the Sanskrit alphabet...words bring concept and vibration and form into being...within the Silence of stilled mind they are torn asunder...the great darkness that is traversed is the ego...The Mother of the Universe, and in utter submission, The Mother liberates and the dream is known as it is...

19.   I understand that SELF is separate, untouched, pure...I also understand it is the ego playing these games. But in our case it seems to continue...How so? Remedy?

G: Don't attach to it...when there are no desires it will settle...when you are in the moment there will be no attachment to...when you seek nothing whatever rises is as it is...

20.   I guess kundalini awakening is a synonym to Self-Realization?

G: No - It can help in the process. But it can also take one down a long road on many other journeys first. It does not always lead to Self-Realization. It is a falsehood that when kundalini reaches the crown chakra, Self-Realization takes place. First it must come back to the heart. It must rest in the heart. The surrender must be complete. The searching ends and Self-Realization is entered into at that point. As long as the mind keeps seeking, the continuing phenomena will happen; visions, lights, sounds, siddhis, etc. etc. But when the heart is entered into and the seeking ends then Grace descends and Self-Realization or Enlightenment takes place. The other happenings help to purify and move conscious awareness towards being ready to accept that Divine Grace. To ultimately surrender all experience and concepts and self ideations to the altar of truth and be willing to enter into the great unknown and unknowable. It is a process of preparation. It prepares one for Self-Realization. To move beyond the physical and subtle realms into the Reality which makes the other realms possible. When you have searched the physical and the subtle...have seen how things may be manipulated and how powers come and go and that in the end they in themselves are not enlightening nor do they bring the peace nor Bliss that lasts...then you are ready to utterly surrender. When the heart is entered and surrender is complete the Enlightenment or Self-Realization happens by Grace. When all of the doing has been done. And all of the searching comes to an end and surrender happens then Divine Grace takes over...

21. After I wrote I thought to share with you also the experience of feeling energetically rebuilt on a (sub) cellular level - and was wondering if you ever experienced this.

G: Don't concern yourself with all of that...it has nothing to do with the real you in the end. The body comes and goes. You are not touched by any of these seeming unfolding events. Including all of the kundalini activity. In the end the Self is unchanging. These appear to be quite real happenings but just let them unfold and see the Source from where they are emerging. Go to the root not the by-product. But indeed one does go through a cellular cleansing.

22. I have literally been seeing all life as Light for a period. Once the energy resides in the heart and rests there, does one always exist in these communion Samadhi states, and visually perceive the Light? - it all seems too powerful to be able to reside in at all times.

G: The Samadhi state has nothing to do with perceiving Light. Light is a manifestation of energy. Moving Consciousness. In the end you are within a still state.

Samadhi is being in touch with the Self. When you touch the Self the Bliss states will be known. When you reach the Self there is no big perception of Light or Dark. Those are still of mind and aspect. Subtle aspect. There is further to go. When you let go of the phenomena and trace back the self to Source then this overwhelming will end. There will be Peace and Bliss and Absolute Pristine Awareness.

23.   Is transcendence somehow a natural product of Nirvikalpa? Or might I live this incarnation without resting in the Sahaja silence that you speak of?

G: When experiencing the Nirvikalpa State there are three things that may emerge...
1. The mind and thought and body are once again accepted as the reality and then the Nirvikalpa becomes just another experience...a concept that is gravitated to...
2: Sahaja Sarvikalpa Samadhi remains...in this avenue there is some body awareness and the intermittent thought which rises but neither are clung to... for they are known to be empty in nature and therefore Non-Dual...so the Non-Dual state is maintained. Or;
3: Nirvikalpa Sahaja Samadhi continues on in which no thoughts rise...there is ever the Silent Awareness of Non-Dual Being...

24.   What about fear and raging mind?

G: The fears and thoughts rise and keep coming until they clear...then simply clarity will remain. This is why you must stay centered within the Heart. The Heart of Being will see you through this amazing journey. It is now in the process of showing you what you are not. And to show you that all that is rising is due to mind and thought. The illusive and illusion of it all. This, is what is the value in what is happening. But yes, it appears to have substance and be real at the time...but it only has the reality that you give it. That you cling to. The main thing is to not 'fear' what is happening...the fear in itself will generate like thoughts and happenings...so come to center...and be Still...just sit and go within...Be Still...yes, in the beginning the mind will rage...it is the accumulated garbage which surfaces and shows itself at first...but it WILL Clear...just have patience...this is why it has been stated in the teachings that an external Guru is needed...to help to support you during this important time... to help to point the way through...this is the sword of spiritual realm...it cuts ego and brings life and death within the same blow...Enlightenment is being blown out...so be prepared for the wild ride in the beginning...in the end is Bliss and Peace...so hang in there...

25.   How are the ancient patterns gone beyond?

G: Patterns once again are empty illusions of misidentifications. So what remains? Like a stick cutting water, Essence can never be divided.

26.   I read your email on Nad. I have questions concerning this. How does one know that this sound that one hears all the time, but more especially when there is silence, is Nad and not some medical problem like tinnitus? I hear this high pitch sound all the time, especially in my right ear, it becomes very loud when silence abounds, sometimes so loud I can't sleep. When I apply yoni mudra during meditation it changes slightly, it becomes like (hard to describe accurately) a siren or flute.

G: Indeed dear One, in the fact that during the yoni mudra it merges into a flute-type sound once again only establishes that it is indeed the Nad or universal sound within that is heard and not a 'medical' condition... so continue on and be at peace...just rest in the silence which the sound rides upon...the sound is the moving conscious energy...the silence is the stilled Constant...

Yes indeed sometimes the sound can be overpowering but it is simply an indication that you are on the right track...this One also had such a manifestation and can say that it will settle in time into the ongoing Silence or Mouni state...the Nad will help to stay your focus beyond the mentations of mind...

27.   I have also seen various forms of light during meditation. Mostly I see purple and sometimes I see a dark spot with a golden halo (like a solar eclipse) other times (not often) I see a point of light and of course I see black space most often.

G: These plays of light will come and go... and in the end they have no great significance except to point to some part of conscious awareness that is being tapped into...or some nadi or channel that is being traversed...within the great Universe within...so do not cling to any of these outer phenomena as anything other than outer signposts along the way...they are not the destination...they are simply scenic happenings along the way...

28.　I guess my question really is, what are the signposts of true yoga and should they be held to or let go?

G: The only Goal is Self-Realization...in breaking through the conditionings and illusions and delusions...so just continue on and see these as simply signposts along the way... and do not follow any of them...continue on until the ego self reaches the implosion and dissolution into the Universal Self of Being...some think that they have reached but they have only gone down another of Maya's paths of illusion...so continue on...but it is well that you send the updates as you may be guided as to what is the true experience...and when it is time to surrender all...

29.　By far my best meditations occur when I feel almost no need to breathe at all. It has happened to me several times now where I don't have need to breathe for seconds - this is wonderful when it happens.

G: Yes...at these times you can be drawn inward...that is true...but eventually we do not wish to cling to the ideation that these states must be accessed only through the meditational means...eventually these may become Sahaja...or effortlessly ongoing...once the identification is broken through and the Nirvikalpa Samadhi is entered...it may indeed, with proper guidance, go into a Sahaja Nirvikalpa Samadhi which is ongoing...and from that point there is meditation without meditating...it will be the natural state of being beyond minds' interference...

Mouni - silent and stilled mind within the natural Samadhi state of Being...

30.   I lived on almost nothing, roaming about the world dysfunctional and ill. And in a panic, praying and trusting in all my concepts hahaha. I heard my mind breaking apart like an iceberg cracking apart in the ocean. I saw my mind melt away like wax melting on a candle. I had Ramana's experience and died to myself, and a short time later, a gripping like a fist came out of pure intelligence and ME was back.

G: ah...you have taken back mind...that is all...if you have tasted the freedom then you KNOW that it is Truth...THAT cannot be denied...read *the Viveka-chudamani*[6] as it speaks on this...do not take back the mind again...and then once again start clinging to the emotions etc...let it go...you can...if you have had the experience then you know on One level that you as personality do not exist except as the concepts and mind thoughts that you entertain and hold...but these are not the Purity of Being...ego-identification as body - mind - and form are once again attempting to gain soil and sprout...but the Truth has been entered...so let it go...be the child of the Universe...why to cling to such pain?

31.   The pain was excruciating for thirty years and only recently has it let up. But I am afraid at any moment the suffering and mental craziness, heat, illnesses, and millions of totally alien experiences will come back.

G: This 'fear' is what is ruling you...yet it only has the substance that you yourself give it... if you give it no energy it WILL dissipate...Essence is Eternally the Same...Pure and beyond the contamination of experience in form...so why to seek out these fears? You have crossed the biggest unknown and unknowable into the great mystery... why do you take back the identification with the transient as being the absolute? The transient is just that...transient...the Absolute is what you are...beyond any of these temporary identifications...fears come from what *may* come...why to fear what is not even here? Bring yourself back to this moment...

---

[6] Viveka-chudamani *translated by A J Alston, Shanti Sadan, London 1977*

81

32. I have been meditating for some time, and now when I open my eyes and blink, I see a blue circle surrounded by golden ring. What does this mean and is it possible to see this all the time?

G: It could be what is termed the blue pearl...it is a connecting with God energy...but do not get caught up in this phenomena...it is better that you continually seek what is the Source of your being...and cut through all the phenomena for the Truth that underlies ALL of creation.

33. What about all the strange dreams coming? Snakes and Fires and many other things.

G: Yes, the dreams of Snakes of every size and variety may arise...along with fires and flying and churches...many variations...and the dreams appear to be quite real...Lucid dreams may occur and many with a lot of symbolism - especially religious...even past-life events may start being seen...Just don't panic... they will eventually subside...and don't run yourself ragged attempting to 'figure out' just what they are showing you...just know that it is a byproduct of the kundalini phenomena show...

There may also be dreams of vehicles and of falling...Sometimes there can be quite a show for quite sometime...and in the midst of a large upheaval don't be surprised if regular photographs start having some quite strange images, lights, shadows etc. appearing...eventually it will subside...just know that it is transient and don't give it too much importance...

34. On reported experience of deception among healers:

Most are not out to actively deceive you...the ones involved in the deception are themselves, deluded...this delusion carries over into their actions...they are attempting to bring you into their perceived illusions of truth... their distortions...although they believe that they are helping – such is the delusion of maya...Until one has completed and has reached beyond the maya realam and has successfully integrated Shiva/Shakti...or come to "know" and rest within the constant...only when one has transcended the duality into the non-dual...when one has gone from the personal to the impersonal...only when one's own illusions of truth have been utterly shattered to where they no longer exist...only when the Truth of Being is reached...only THAT ONE is ready to guide and point the way to liberation to anyone else...Anyone that is still in suffering cannot hand happiness or Bliss of Self to anyone else...one that is still in theory cannot give experience...

35. I want to activate the kundalini to feel completely self-empowered and unlimited in my potential. And then I want to manifest some of my potential. My short term goal is to achieve some success with my work and relationships.

G: Success has nothing to do with the exteriors...and what is self-empowerment? That once again is ego-based desire - to 'BE' something...you already are all that you need to be...This is once again an ego-based desire. More control...you equate more energy with more control...but this energy is NOT controlled...it controls you...so once again this is NOT the way...in the end the most control is when nothing is controlled but simply seen as the natural flow and progression of this life's being...that is all...and you move forward for this moment alone...not projecting into the future...nor clinging to the past...they have no relevance in the Now...be in this moment what you are...that is all...

36. I feel trapped by limiting beliefs and habits that I cannot seem to get rid of. I figured Kundalini might be a way through these problems.

G: Absolutely not... you break through the identifications through self-contemplation...by seeing absolutely that you are not the body, nor mind, nor emotions...not by creating energy which only intensifies the body and subtle body identifications...While kundalini creates a moving consciousness...it is in the end, once again based on the transients...anything that is moving is transient...and not the Constant which is beyond all form and movement...you do not reach the seed or Source by moving anywhere...it is only when the kundalini has completed its course and once again rests within the heart that the Constant is Known...and that can take 'lifetimes'...not simply days, months or even years...it is not a quick fix path...

37.   My potential range of behaviors and actions seem limited by fears and belief systems I am having a lot of difficulty ridding myself of. I can feel the energy and belief inside in some latent state. Occasionally it surfaces but I feel as though there's some sort of emotional/mental cage holding it all down - refusing to let me reap the benefits of the potential in us all.

G: You are right in seeing the mind as the culprit...the misidentifications...this creates the barriers...the perceived suffering and negative values...what needs to be broken through is mind-thought identifications...you do not need to have more created within the kundalini phenomena that naturally arise within this context...There is in the end no more gain...nor lack of energy...it is only your perception that creates this illusion...the Source is Always the same and stable in nature...and you are That...

38.   The more I meditate, the more I'm beginning to think it has something to do with the belief system/energy behavior patterns my parents instilled in me (probably without their being aware of doing so). Anyhow, it seems to me that energy is the key to everything and by activating energy it will provoke clearer thought and pave the way for more courageous and natural action. So this is why I think Kundalini might be the answer. I feel energy blockages and by practicing Kundalini I may succeed in removing these, no?

G: Energy blockages are mind blockages...they are stagnations...they are when something is being resisted...fought against...when acceptance is not there...let go of the resistances...embrace life at its core...and do the Self-Enquiry...just live life in the moment...cherish each moment that arises...as it is simply the unfolding of past karma created happenings...and your action and re-action set up the next patterns that will emerge...that is all...Surrender all to the

84

Universe...and it will work out...just go forward in Trust...our lives are perfect as they are in bringing forth the wisdom that is sought...find the still center within...and you will find that there is no longer a within or a without...that ALL of creation is part and parcel of your Being...

39. Can one relate to the future/destiny by Kundalini Yoga?

G: If you are asking about paranormal happenings within the kundalini experience...yes, these things occur within the kundalini experience...but they do not in the end give you anymore power or peace or control...in controlling one thing you lose control of another... it remains in balance...your destiny is created by what your actions and re-actions are within this moment...if life is lived well NOW...you need not worry or be concerned with what is beyond NOW...

40. How does one find a right Guru?

G: Find One that moves your spirit to Silence to Peace...One that is readily available to answer questions as they arise... Do not gravitate to any that give initiations and then leave you to simmer on the back burner so to speak...in olden days the Guru was served by the chelas...it was not that he needed their service...it was so that they were living around in close proximity...not just going to a seminar here and there...if you want simply a good Teacher that you can glean something from...then go to One that gives you tools to move towards center and silence and peace...which is not to say one that sits and feeds your ego...getting a big head while, in the beginning, seems to lead to peace and joy in the end it only brings a bigger disaster...And when you find your Guru...give them the respect due...but do not expect them to run your entire life... the mindset you enter and the actions and re-actions that occur, you must live with...so use wisdom - do not follow blindly...it is only by direct experience that you Know anything...not by concepts and conjectures that the teacher speaks - no matter how grand...

41. After initiation does the Shakti stay active all the time?

G: It is moving within its own timing...sometimes more active - sometimes it appears to rest...but it is always there...

42. I feel incredibly lightheaded/spacey all the time. Sometimes this intensifies to a point where I feel as if I will fly out of my body, disappear, die, fade into nothingness.

G: Well first of all, are you a vegetarian? Sometimes a heavier diet is needed to ground one...also while this may feel quite disconcerting at the moment - once again relax...you will not fly out of your body nor be lost into the void...and in the end what you experience is exactly this 'nothingness'...although it is not a nothingness as you may expect...but the Core of Life...Pregnant with ALL that will ever be within the transient universe...the Core of your identity or life Being is simply This...there is once again nothing to fear...it is this fear of the loss of self which is difficult to transcend...for we have taken ourselves to be this stable mass of flesh and thought, etc...when we are anything but in the final analysis...we are Eternal Primal Essence that has no individual self-identity at core...one day you will indeed experience Enlightenment or Realization... and will Know the Truth of Being and Life within the Constant/Transient....

43. I feel surges of energy rushing out of my head/leaking out. This is accompanied by a feeling that everything is insubstantial.

G: Yes...all is empty in nature...like the dream at night... appearing to be quite real until you awaken in the morning...what you are starting to experience is equal to this...but instead of seeing it only within the Dream State...you are starting to awaken to the reality that it is also so within Life as it is... and indeed it is... but there is nothing to fear...but know that the Dream never touches the Eternal Core Purity of Being...it is a transient happening which allows for the experience of touch, taste, duality, interaction, emotional experience and response such as love, compassion and all the various and sundry experiences termed 'life'.

44. I feel dead, totally emptied out, body feels like an object - as dead as a table.

G: Yes, have also experienced this feeling... the body is an object...it is not who you are...and it is a disconcerting feeling when it happens...but when you enter finally into Realization or Enlightened Awareness it will pass...you will 'normalize', so to speak...not that this is abnormal...it is a part of the process of unraveling what you are not...you are not the physical form...it is a vehicle... this part of the process is very difficult...when you feel like a walking zombie...but it will get better...that I can promise you...there is resurrection coming...just hang in there...I am so happy that you have written...for your experience is one that this One has already traveled...and can absolutely state that it will end within a triumph of Spirit... and Freedom...

45. I feel as though I am 'inside' other people. Pick up thoughts that seem not to be mine. Like murderous, angry, evil feelings.

G: Yes, also this is the empathic connection...you become very sensitive and can pick up unintentionally - like a mirror of others' reflections...feeling their physical and emotional bodies...and sometimes it is difficult to distinguish whether it is your own feeling or someone else's...and this is in place to show you that we are inherently All only ONE Being...the only thing that separates us is the mind...when that starts to become more fluid you will indeed find that you are linked absolutely with the rest of the chain of Creation...for at the heart of it All is simply the ONE Primal Essence or Core Life Substance...and you are THAT minus the personal identity...

46. I hear voices which mock, condemn, swear, belittle.

G: Yes...this is all of our own insecurities which fly in our faces...they appear to manifest quite real as these disembodied voices...but it will end...once you see through the illusion of it...that you are not these misidentifications...when you get over and through what you have thought you are not...and all the vain imaginings and fears we have held throughout the ages...all of these may appear until you see through them as simply mind-generated fear and insecurities...falsehoods of identifications and fears unfounded...these will indeed end...just once again see them for what they are.

47. Moments of clairvoyance

G: Yes, subtle realms entered...but do not cling to any of these transient unfoldings...

48. a) I was wondering if you were familiar with Susan Segal and her history.

G: Yes, absolutely...

> b) It seemed to me like she may have had a kundalini crisis but it was so powerful that it permanently knocked her spiritual body out of alignment with her physical body. Do you think there is a way to bring the two back into alignment in her type of case?

G: It wasn't a kundalini crises at all...it was a movement into what is beyond the transient. In her case there was a disturbance due to not having foundational knowledge or understanding what was taking place...this is why the external Guru is needed...someone that has already traversed this experience and understands what is going on...and can help One to stabilize within this new Reality...it can be quite unnerving to go from at first witnessing the body and mind to a total loss of self...but this is what Enlightenment entails...Enlightenment means 'Blown Out' and that is indeed what happens...there was no crisis in her case other than not understanding the process of Self-Realization...or what is termed Source - Brahman - Essence or Self... if she had come in contact with someone that understood much earlier on, it would have settled much sooner into the bliss and peace.

49. I feel like I am going crazy and wonder how much the human brain can take before it goes crazy.

G: All of these processes and experiences are, in the end, to show you that all is created and sustained by mind...that the transient is transparent and empty in nature...the problem happens when you cling to the experiences and want them to make 'sense' within what is termed the 'normal' life...this all happens to, in the end, get you to break through all the identifications...this is why I stress doing Self-Enquiry to break through the illusions more rapidly and safely...rather than having everything appearing to manifest in your face point blank so to speak...it is not the human brain that causes the problem...it is the egoic identification with the transient as being the permanent...with the self being a compilation of the body - mind - conditioned experience within the terms and context called 'this lifetime'...all of this proceeds to take you to discover the Timeless Source which makes the play of the so-called individual possible...and shows you what you are not in the end...

First you find out what you are not...then you may be freed to discover what you are...

50.   I feel there is only one intention behind everyones' wish to awaken the Kundalini i.e. for Self-Realization or Enlightenment.

G: Yes...but to many, being Realized or Enlightened has many different ideations and concepts attached to it...that is why there is an attempt on this end to clarify just what is wanted...for many have the misguided ideation that when one is Realized or Enlightened that their life is full of mystical happenings...that one 'controls the world', that they have the ability to wave a magic wand so to speak...that they become a caricature of the 'enlightened master'...it, for many, is more of an 'ego trip' rather than a sincere longing for the Truth to be revealed...this is not to imply that you are on an ego trip... not at all... it is simply said to have one look at their intentions and motivations and what they entail...truthfully...

51.   Do I not need any Guru for initial Kundalini yoga? I am aged forty-seven. Being born in South Indian orthodox Brahmin family, I do puja in the morning and night, read *Upanishads*, attend Satsang etc.

G: It matters not your station nor caste...in fact the sooner you throw away those identifications the better...as far as kundalini yoga don't get caught up in another 'practice'...if you are seeing the sounds and experiencing the Nad then there is already an awakening...the Yogas all interconnect and overlap...you may start within one but by the end of your journey you will have entered into All...you have been initiated into the five names etc. and so indeed have already been initiated into that practice...it is not specifically called such but in the end that is what it is...you are also now in touch with this one and therefore are once again having that link...if your heart reaches out in devotion to any guru you will not be rejected...it is your heart which keeps and maintains the connection...unless a guru specifically closes the door and walks away...May the desires of your innermost heart flourish and come to fruition...

52. I think what I am trying to find out is if kundalini is awakened by whatever means, does one continue to have kriyas? Would the kriyas continue for number of years? If you don't have Kriyas continuously, does that mean one's Chitta is not pure? Should one try to do Japa etc., so that the kriyas will continue?

G: You only have spontaneous kriyas when indeed the kundalini is in fact active...the spontaneous kriyas only happen as long as needed...and then they will subside...what needs to be moved is moved...if you do not continue to have kriyas that means that whatever needed to be adjusted has been and that is the end of it...One does not need to do Japas to have the kriyas continue...

53. How can you be sure Shakti has pierced all chakras and if not, how does one achieve Samadhi?

G: You need not worry about attempting to categorize where you are... just continue on in your Sadhana and when you have reached to where you need to be you will indeed be pulled into a State...when enough has been released and when you have surrendered and forgotten the self ego identity you will find that you will enter into a Samadhi...

54. Once the kriyas stop should one continue with normal meditation - meaning closing your eyes and concentrating between two eyes?

G: You should stay within the awareness of the heart...the spiritual heart of Being...that is where the journey will end...from that point the last will be found...the one that does not bring back the ego identification...

55.   I read that one should fix the mind on one's own self. How does this work? Is this a simple method to practice?

G: Keep bringing everything back to: what is the source of this I?...what is the source of this experience?...look at everything that you 'think' makes up your identity...and then see if it is transitory...if it is transitory, how can it be the Eternal One or Source?...you are the I...what is this I?...question it...until the identifications are broken through and only the Source remains and then surrender...

56.   I have recently gone back, with some reluctance I have to say, to eating meat. I have some guilt about this but have to admit I feel much better and stronger both physically and mentally. I feel far more grounded and balanced and for me this is/has been a rare thing. What are your thoughts on this - in your view is it okay to eat meat or am I committing spiritual suicide here?!

G: Yes...the high protein can most definitely help within the grounding. As far as the other is concerned...there are two things to consider...from the Absolute standpoint nothing is born and nothing dies... death is relative to the physical form alone...and ALL within the universe contain consciousness...even plants...to those that have no mind gravitating to killing and anger and if you are not identifying with the death of something...then there is no karmic debt or problem with meat eating...to those that come from a cultural background of vegetarianism; or if you have changed your religion to one that prohibits the eating of meat; or if you have such a strong mindset against it then to that one it is a sin...sin and right and wrong are views of culture and mind... if you are not involved in hunting and killing as sport with the end to inflict pain then there is no problem in the eating of meat...plants have also been shown to have fear responses...it matters not in the end and one life form is not higher than another ALL come from the same Core Essence or Source...Everything within this realm is transient...

57. I'd like to say I still drink and smoke herb off and on. I can handle those recreationally just fine, I've found my 'questioning myself and reality' occurs when I try 'energetical exercises', for things usually occur. But without the foundation being rock solid, like you said.

G: You may think you are handling it fine...but you may find that down the road you are not...and then it is too late in the process to turn around and go the other way... of course you have the right to live your life however you so choose...as it is you that must live within the consequences...but I advise caution within this area...due to the drugs many get 'stuck' within a certain level or experience...and find it difficult to extricate themselves and do not understand why they are not progressing in the end...

58. Daily emotions, disturbances don't seem to touch me now. I am trying to keep my mind (physical) as calm as possible.

G: Good but don't attempt to repress the mind...see through it and it will settle naturally when it is given no more energy to feed on...otherwise you do not reach to the pregnant void of Source...but simply the void of devoid...

59. I saw myself rising. I noticed that my body was stationary but I was out of my body(maybe my consciousness was out). I could not feel my body and any parts of it. I did not know what to do...

G: hahahahahaha...there is nothing to do but to simply see that consciousness does not reside within the body form... and that the body is simply a tool...a vehicle of experience...

60. I have been practicing breath techniques for two years now. I feel energy movements and heat in the spine and head, and I hear some sound frequencies. But in a very feeble way, no great experiences or energy upsurges - do you think this is kundalini?

G: It might just be pranic surges created by extended breath work...if there are no other accompanying phenomena or activities...

61. I have read some scientific reports about brain and consciousness, and this stuff is really troubling my mind. You know science says, "Brain activity produces consciousness". Do you have some insight about this?

G: They are 100% backwards. Consciousness creates brain activity...as the consciousness changes indeed the brain changes...more connections are made...balance happens...the brain is simply like a switch board...but it does not create consciousness...it is like a computer...there must be something that indeed programs it...it holds and stores and moves electrical impulses within the physical form...but it does not create consciousness.

62. About snakes in dreams. I saw one and it was very, very real. That night I forgot everything (dreams) but this one remained. I did not mention this earlier. It was about a snake which entered my home. My mother and father panicked as I was too close to the snake. I told them that everything would be alright and I guided the snake back to its hole and everything was fine... it's funny...but another experience... hahaha

G: hahahahahaha... yes... this is also understood...it shows that indeed the kundalini is manifesting within the 'right' mode...that it is being guided and pulled in the right direction...you are lucky to be progressing within a stable mode...you were right not to panic and to simply guide it to where it belongs gently...wonderful...this is why it is important to have an awakening under the guidance of a completed guru...and to relax within the whole experience...to work on the subtle levels of awareness and mind which in the end are the sole aim of kundalini...to move one into alignment with the Truth of Being...

63. I have a couple of questions about the OM.

a) Is there a certain way of going about this practice, for instance (technique)?

G: First begin by intoning it in an extended version...on the sound of the *mmmmmm*... keep it extended and it should create a vibration at the top of the ead...then hear the sound internally...do the OM mentally...not superficially where there are other thoughts competing with it...go into it mentally fully with commitment...OM is the first sound and the last Alpha - Omega...it is the first of creation and the last when entering into the Formless Constant...it is representative of that which is beyond the transient...the Infinite One...

64.   Books can't help me find the truth and I am not sure how to really find the truth in meditation. I feel as if I am at the doorway yet my fear is holding me back. I try to surrender but something is holding me back. I cry just at the thought of being so close yet it feels so far.

G: Yes...the fear is the great fear of ego death...it struggles to maintain its place...feeling that it must control in order to be...but Source or Self is beyond the limited ego...and this feeling of being so close yet so far is known...for this One just before entering into Source there was the last great fear that rose up...then it took a conscious decision that Truth was wanted above all else - even life...the surrender came...and indeed the ego was seen to be the imploded self-identity...it was a set of ideations and identities wrapped around a form...and they were not what remained when all of the concepts etc. were blown out...this is Enlightenment...being Blown Out...it is quite an accurate statement of what occurs within that moment...and what remains is what has always been at the Heart of Being...Freedom is known to have always existed but covered over with mental fabrications and body identity...when the transient is clung to too tightly the Eternal is not known...

65.   I often have to be careful when mediating because the heat becomes so intense. Can you perhaps help me?

G: Meditation should not be a concentrating on something...or attempting to move something...meditation happens naturally when the mind is stilled...and stillness comes with repeated practice until it no longer remains a practice but simply who and what you are...stilled awareness...

66.   I don't care if I'm ever psychic, see auras or anything.

G: Good...because this can be a big trap of ego along the way...people mistake psychic realm - astral realm - subtle experience for an increased spirituality...it is not so...only those that can see beyond this trap will indeed traverse it without getting stuck and caught within that cycle...you are wise to see beyond this...

67.   It's funny, I have had cravings for meat, but don't like the idea of eating something that has been killed.

G: Yes this is understood...but sometimes within this process there comes a need for a grounding...and if the craving is there then there is a need...you do not need to go overboard...try fish...if that does not do it then white meat, if that is still not heavy enough then red meat...you need not eat a large quantity but a little may be needed...remember this that All forms are transient and that in the end Nothing dies...this is not that we should all become big meat eaters...nor cause any suffering...of course we also alleviate suffering as we may...but also know this: even vegetables have consciousness...

68.   I have tried Clonazepam and it does help, but I don't want to use it long term.

G: Yes...good...but it is an okay stabilizer 'when needed'...as the problem has been trauma and until you can break through that mentation that happens then the Clonazepam can help...but do not take it in a regimented fashion...use it sparingly...as needed...as you do not want to create any more toxins than necessary...

69.   Yesterday, I walked on the beach barefoot and it was beautiful.   There's   beauty   and   magic   with   this transformation along with horror and pain.

G: Yes...and this may be used as a practice to enter into NOW...use the beach time or any walking time to become aware of simply what is happening NOW...feel each movement of each step...then be aware simply of the wind on your face...no more and no less...then of the sky, seeing it as it is...start to learn to do this without a mental dialogue going on...bring all your attention to the action...that you may find stillness...it is a Zen way of Being...a natural centering tool...a natural way to begin to learn to enter into a spontaneous ongoing meditation...we'll begin there...do not wish to overload you...or share too much until you can know that I am trustworthy and a teacher that may indeed point you in the direction of Truth and Self-discovery...

70.   Why am I getting so sick? How can I get through this?

G: Remember that kundalini is a cleansing process on all levels; spiritual - mental - physical...and it indeed brings forth all the psychological fears, sadness, pain, etc. that have been part of your make-up for lifetimes...if you can keep this in mind it helps one through the process...it will end...the trick is in learning how to see through the process and the rising mentations, etc...this is where I come in...

71.   On 'higher realms':

You come to this point eventually...we want the mystical, etc. etc...sometimes it takes the hard route of traveling through the mystical to get to where the true mystery is...and that is simply day to day existence...we play the small games until we get to the largest game which is simply the joy and bliss which is life.

72.   I've felt flashes of light go off in my head at night.

G: Yes...this will happen many times when stressed...these flashes will occur...sometimes you may see a circulating light that just shows the energy is cycling...the other comes at times of physical and mental stress...when that happens, back off and rest.

73.   Right now I am feeling completely devoid of energy as if somebody has sucked all the energy from my body...I do not know how I am able to maintain awareness...also the

body is hot and I am sweating (a bit) and I do not feel like thinking...a lot of changes have come.

G: If you need rest then take rest...but most of all continue on to relax within this process...it is still throwing out toxins, etc. You are fine...just don't push the energy factor...if lagging in energy...go out into nature if possible...away from buildings and people as sometimes these may be a bit draining...

74.   A previous teacher who taught kriya yoga, told me that kundalini is always flowing, and that the key is for it to flow faster and faster. Is this true?

G: The key to what? It simply activates all the three bodies into divesting themselves of all the stored information. It doesn't have to do with faster or slower...

75.   Must one always experience the unpleasant side of kundalini prior to an awakening? Is this always a precursor to liberation?

G: It brings up all of your conditionings and belief systems to be looked at and challenged...one can either see it as a negative or a positive.

76.   To date, I really can't say that my experiences have been all that bad and actually, there have been many times where my experiences were very ecstatic. This only changed about five months ago when I started to feel as if I was on an emotional rollercoaster, but even that is balancing out now.

G: For some it is easier than others. Yes, sometimes the experiences can be ecstatic and for some they can have years of bliss before the difficulty begins. Each person navigates it a bit differently...But the main thing is not to get fearful and to stay in a middle path dealing with it.

77.   Do you know why someone who has had awakened kundalini experiences would have frequent intense hot flashes during menopause? This has been going on for

more than two years. Also, do you know why sitting down to meditate causes hot flashes? Or why just typing this email to you is causing me to have one now? (Seriously.)

G: Usually kundalini energy is not reacting as a hot flash but up the spine or as heat in the head or simply a particular area of the body...It could be that you are so sensitive that every burst of heat is intensified at this time...Sitting in meditation can cause a rise in kundalini activity. Sometimes people that connect with me also have an increased activity...But my main guess in this area is that simply due to the kundalini activity as well as hormonal hot flashes you have become so sensitive that one sets off the other...

78. Tell me about how to deal with auditory and visual hallucinations suffered after kundalini awakening. It started after concentrating on the Ajna chakra.

G: Well I am not surprised...Ajna chakra opens one to subtle realm experience...so the first thing is to STOP immediately any third eye meditations...

79. The visual images I see are my own thoughts but I can't stop them. They are images of my favorite deity and saints talking to me. How do I come out of this? The images are seen and thoughts are heard all the time and even when I am not meditating.

G: Then the first step is to realize that they are indeed projections of mind...that they are transient and empty in nature...they have only the reality and substance that you give them. Then don't feed them with any energy at all. Do not run from it nor focus on it...in time it will simply end.

80. Since July I have been very tired and unusually undriven - aside from waking up in the middle of the nights (I resort to 1/2 dosage of Excedrin PM) my symptoms have been disappearing quite quickly - further accelerated when I could finally realign to my true self whose 'voice' has been so indiscernible amongst all the other 'noise' to fully accept that the ego and the imagination created so much of the

symptoms I experience - 'Bodhi tree' syndrome). Man, it was like science fiction and I think I was talking to the wrong people on the way - i.e. your point that the mind will follow a particular viewpoint and create it - man oh man!!!

G: Well now that discovery is a Big step...with that understanding you are at a good place to begin...kundalini is of the consciousness and not the body...the body is a reflection and an outcome...the experience is an outcome...

81.   I am looking for relief with; my feet, lethargy -- lack of disciplines and/or 'umph', concentration and my 'auric winds' so to speak. Do regular Sivananada style yoga every day and that helps -- meditation is not there yet. So...I am wondering...any ideas?

G: Start with the breath....and the mindful walking...one step at a time...don't want to overload you all at once or else nothing gets established right...

82.   Are there any criteria that can be used to distinguish between kundalini symptoms and either medical symptoms or angelic/demonic possession?

G: Kundalini will have many overlapping criteria and symptoms including mental, physical and emotional plus subtle - whereas medical or simply psychological symptoms will stay within a much more limited diagnostic persuasion...look to the symptomology...as far as possession, that is an opening of being influenced by a disincarnate entity... but that can Only happen if you open yourself up to it...Kundalini process can bring up terrors but they are simply fears, and not outwardly chasing after heinous acts... that is the difference...one may have this fear of being possessed but it is simply the fear and not a reality...

83.   What is the purpose of the kundalini activity?

G: To take one to Self-Realization... to clear out all of the conditionings, concepts, and fears...

84. How can I assist the process?

G: By staying relaxed and working on centering activities; by developing the Yogas of Bhakti and Karma by developing mindful awareness; by relaxed breathing to center and release any rising phenomena - do not chase after any siddhis that may arise nor chase after sounds and lights...they may be a focal point but not a goal; by doing Self-Enquiry where you confront your ideations head on by working with a completed teacher.

85. Is there anything that I should not do?

G: Yes, don't fear it, don't attempt to push anything.

86. For the moment, my only instruction is 'just let it happen'.

G: There is a way to let it happen and there is a way to understand and assist its happening - I suggest using the latter.

87. How important is sleep?

G: This is Extremely Important. You Must get to bed early otherwise the system can become severely and overtaxed. In order to stay in balance you cannot overtax the system, it needs time to relax...

88. All my conceptual mind up to date is being 'defragmented' and in the process of being redefined but it's so darn subtle to grasp...

G: Don't define. Don't Grasp. It will expand and contract then simply one day Grace will come and all the conceptualizing will be blown away. Do not strive in effort, relax into seeing. See what IS from what appears in a coloration. The coloration is a falsity so let it go...it is a past tape, a reflection...all reflection is past - is subject and object - beyond reflection is clear seeing...

89. The energies around me seem more intense at night when I am sleeping. I have been waking up between 2am and 4am for the past several nights because of these sensations. Particularly the ones in my lower abdomen. There has

been some mild heat throughout my belly, as well as elsewhere. I've been getting out of bed and going outside so that I don't think about it so much. Then, I just go back to bed.

G: So when this happens just sit and go into the relaxed breathing...close the eyes and simply become aware of the moment. Don't chase after the phenomena, just go into stillness. It is quite often that those in a kundalini process wake up around 3am or so...it is a good quiet time for meditation so just go into the breath and let the mind still then go back to sleep...

90.   I have found myself with access to a lot of teachers, channels and the like.

G: Channels once again are not the best way. Just because something is discarnate it does not mean that it is any higher or more knowledgeable. One can encounter some very nasty things being opened to channeling and what appears to be healthy in the end can in turn wreck havoc with one's mind...it doesn't matter if it were a pure channel - in whatever is being said in simply once again another theory until one finds out and experiences it firsthand for themselves...

91.   I started to have very intense meditations, seeing my body as an empty black void filled with space, (meditating in a mirror was suggested to me before this).

G: While an interesting phenomenom, it is not an experience of what is termed 'the Absolute' or 'Void' - this was an internal experience of simply a limited space within a certain structure or form. Stay away from the mirror - all of these things have nothing to do with finding the truth within - they are chasing phenomena and occult and paranormal avenues that is not a higher path nor one that will lead one to Self-Realization...

92.   What is Enlightenment anyway, and do I need to have the kundalini a certain way?

G: The whole thing is to merge Shiva and Shakti or the seen and unseen, the movement into stillness, the phenomenal into the

Absolute, Duality into Non-Duality. When that is done successfully, 0 point balance remains and the kundalini is stilled. Until then it will continue to bring up everything pushed down and hidden...all concepts...out in the light to be seen and let go of.

Kundalini puts everything right in your face until you deal with it and see beyond what it is showing. It moves through seven levels of awareness. Forget chakras. Look at it as levels of awareness - it is easier to comprehend that way. It might swing from one extreme to the other, from the positive of the awareness to the negative. The thing is to see through the longstanding illusions of truth or non-liberating conditionings that have been taken on, to see through to the inherent nature from which they arise. When this is done successfully then one is pulled into enlightenment and all the falsehoods and conditionings are blown out. Enlightenment means just this: BLOWN OUT.

Self-Realization is simply seeing the Essence beyond the limited ego self. Seeing the True Self versus the constructed self-idea.

93.   What is a living Sadhana?

G: Sadhana is your spiritual practice...What I term living Sadhana is when you no longer have a daily practice of an hour or so of set time...but when your spiritual practice becomes part of your normal ongoing daily life...in this way your normal way of living changes as you progress and everything is integrated as you move through the experience...

94.   What about external religious practices or New Age affirmations? I guess I should ask: what do I do? I feel comfortable living my life without a lot of overt spirituality in it, I get sort of nervous when people are talking about it and all, I dunno, you are a teacher I guess, so perhaps you do. I get turned off by some of the more 'purple power' stuff. I am very down to earth gal.

G: hahahahahahaha... I can assure you no New Age Purple Power spoken here at all and I am also very down to earth. I do not float above the ground hahahaha nor is there a need for gravitating to a lot of overt spirituality (religious dogma and ceremony)...what I work with is the truth beyond all dogma... I do not speak locked into any one religious persuasion. If someone is Hindu and wants to develop some practices it is fine - or Buddhist or Christian - that is a personal preference. But it is not needed. For some it brings a comfort level and that is fine but it is not stressed...for some an outer religious ritual may be grounding and if it brings you a sense of focus and stabilization then great, go for it...

95.   Where I'm at now: Sad, profoundly sad. And when I manage to get past sadness, lonely. I often feel that I've died, and now I have to play the 'game' before I can move on. But I'm tired of the game. I'm just tired to the core.

G: Good, then get good and ready to really look at yourself and the mind games see where they come from and the only one chasing after them is yourself...no one can force you to chase after the mind...if you are tired of the game then you will be ready to go towards liberation without fail. That is what it takes. Getting good and tired of it...

96.   Why does life feel so hard?

G: Because you keep clinging to the pain...

97. Why is it always so lonely?

G: Because you don't want to befriend yourself...

98.   Is this a continuous process for humans? Do we ever becoming 'fully' awakened, or is everything just a stage of the journey?

G: There is Awakening, Self-Realization or Enlightenment and that is a one time happening...once Known it is known but the Transient experience just continues on...it is ever unfolding...

99.   I am wondering about nutrition. I do, at times, cut down immensely on meals, and at times do twenty-four hour

fasts, with food supplements and sufficient water. Doing this makes me feel very good. Please comment as to why this is so! I am losing very, very little weight and am fifteen pounds overweight as is.

G: You may be flushing and keeping the toxins down this way...so it is fine but once again Moderation is the key. When the body is kept without a lot of old stale food in the system you cut down on the toxins and also the body is working less...it is not having to expend so much energy on processing... hence you feel better...

100. Very often some Masters keep saying: "the body does not exist", "there is no body" and similar expressions - among many; Nisargadata and Sri Ramana Marharshi. On one hand, when they spoke those words, they were in a physical human body form... as seen by those attending the talk; they may have not had awareness of their body but that did not make it disappear.

G: This is true...there is consciousness and there is the transient form...the form depends on consciousness but consciousness does not depend on the heavy physical form...They were speaking from their living awareness which was of being simply Non-Dual Consciousness.

101. I experienced on many occasion this state of no awareness of not only the physical form, but of the physical and subtle realm altogether although the body, 'my body', was busy doing some traveling with others, eating, talking, meditating and even giving precise instructions on how to practice mantra meditation. It is possible to assume that, in these moments, if someone would have asked a question to that nature I would have answered that the body did not exist, that nothing exists, but I would not have known what I would have answered, not even being a witness of what was going on during these experiences that lasted many hours. Can you explain?

G: There are many, many levels of conscious awareness...during the process, moments of missing time may occur...others see us speaking and talking etc. but within our own awareness there is no cognition of what took place...I have also had such occurrences but this is a transitional state...

102. As it seems, nothing exists, at least in those kind of sequences of moments. Can you tell if this state is something that could become permanent? It would make a curious world having humans running around their usual life and not being aware of it! Maybe the answer is that it is exactly what is happening, most are just dreaming that there is a world in which they are playing a role (even at being Guru...) while really nothing is happening at all! Comments are welcome since this is still part of my 'unexplained' experiences.

G: No, there comes with Self-Realization cognition of the transient (empty in nature) and the Non-Dual as they are not two. Neither may it really be said that they are ONE. There is just no way for the divisionary vocabulary to express the reality and paradigm that is lived ... For some, like Sri Ramana Maharshi and Nisargadatta, they lived forever in the Nirvikalpa Sahaja Samadhi state of simply negating the physicality of form...Although there was some awareness of it... they still felt pain etc. but having no attachment to bodily form and being in the living nature of the world as simply moving consciousness, it is stated that they are without body and form...

103. How does one awaken kundalini safely and easily?

G: The best way is simply by honest dedication to the spiritual path and by being around a kundalini completed Guru...

104: How does one know by themselves or through others, whether one is awakened?

G: It is best to ask your Guru about this...they will take your experiences and then let you know what is happening...

105. Is spontaneous awakening possible without the intense experiences?

G: If you are speaking about Self-Realization then it is possible...if you are speaking about kundalini then most encounter quite dramatic journeys...

106. Connection of Enlightenment with kundalini. Can one be either without being the other?

G: Kundalini is simply moving consciousness. Enlightenment is the blowing out of the conditionings...Kundalini helps one to see in a more dynamic manner what is being confronted and the illusory nature of mind, the creator of experience...

107. How does one know which level one has reached in kundalini?

G: It doesn't matter what level one is operating in... it is more important to just keep doing the Self-Enquiry or Neti-Neti and breath work until it all blows out...All levels are still within the paradigm of duality...

108. Does kundalini, once activated, take the persons' evolution to the best possible level in everyone?

G: No...not if one is chasing personal powers and occult paranormal experiences...Then one just gets drawn deeper into minds' illusive play...It has nothing to do with Self-Realization...

109. Does giving up our fixed beliefs make kundalini awakening smooth always?

G: No...Kundalini helps one to break out of their belief systems...

110. How does kundalini awakening benefit a person?

G: It puts one in the position of wanting to get out of Maya no matter what the cost...it is the great incentive to reach Realization...The only end of kundalini is to reach Realization and then Shakti is merged in Shiva...

111. I once read something - that the memory losses that can be symptoms of kundalini could have something to do with it, as if a 'separation' of one's own past, with all the problems rooted within that past, is necessary. A consequence of this could be a different 'energy signature' ('frequency signature').

G: Memory losses do occur...nothing to stress about...it will all adjust...what needs to remain will remain...what doesn't simply goes...but time losses also may occur along the way...don't worry about energy signatures...everything within the transient universe is composed of moving and vibrating energy...it is constantly in flux...you are what you are.

112. Mentally, I feel at a loss at times - as well as emotionally; I feel sad at times that I am going on a different path - away from everything I have held onto, yet underneath it all I feel the pull of the path ahead of me...

G: You either want to cling to the past or to let it go and move on... It will adjust however need be, but attempting to cling to any shred of it simply creates that desire; and thus coming with desires not met is suffering and pain...Change is not pain...non-acceptance of change causes the pain...

113. What do you do when the mind questions what to think, as if it is emptying out and frightened of not having anything to think?

G: Let it go...when thought ends there is just simply a gentle peace that remains...What is lost in the unproductive mind drama...The ability to think is not lost...So simply let go...

114. What is the cause of the dream state Maya realm?

G: The cause of this dream? Why must there be a cause? It is Self-exploration and play...What is love? etc. When only the One which is not the One but the Emptiness of Being exists in its separateness...it is love that manifests as the various seeming forms...desire creates the forms and sustains the worlds...any time desire arises then ego form will come into being...

115. Can you split a second in eternity?

G: Now as for eternity...eternity sets up once again a boundary...there is no such boundary...That Which Is...the Formless Constant... the Essence of Being is never born nor has ever died...although all existence is permeated by Being...Being is not in truth touched by so-called existence at all...When you go from the duality of time to the timeless state - as when Realization is perceived; (in that split second) that which is called a 'state' is not a state at all for states are of mind and Realization is beyond mind entirely...words of duality cannot convey the exact ramifications of Truth of the Non-Dual...

116. We all live within the same world... So what is Maya and illusions of truth?

G: All Maya realm experience is unique to you alone...Each person views reality of the Maya realm from their conditionings...Two can face the same circumstances and have totally different experiences....There are as many illusions of truth as there are people...Only when mind and thought and conditionings are dropped and you go beyond division and personality and aspects is the experience the same...

117. What is this 'Self' in Self-Realization?

G: When I speak of the Self I do not speak of the ego self...I speak of That Which is the Formless Constant which is beyond all division and time etc...So when I say to be in the Now... if you are truly in the Now then you will be reaching to the state of Anand...or the beginning of where the opening to Realization is...When the mind is silent with no thought then the Anand or Bliss will rise of its own accord... You will then be in the natural Sahaja state... and from there you proceed on to Realization or Enlightenment...Which is not something that may be attained or obtained as it is the natural state... It is a process of letting go…not creating more...

118. Can Enlightenment or Advaita Be Learned and Proven?

G: People always wish to obtain Enlightenment like they obtain a degree... but this is a path of simplicity itself...only in the utmost simplicity will you realize That Which Is...Realization is simply awakening to the Truth of Being...Which is beyond all concepts and ideations which belong to the world of Maya and change and mind... Therefore you cannot get there by intellectual means...In Kundalini the process is that of dispelling ignorance not gaining more 'relative knowledge'...

119. Is Self-Realization an 'Altered State'?

G: From your point of view it would be an altered state...but it is now my only so-called 'state'...Once these false notions and conditionings drop you don't pick them up again. And at that time (when so-called 'Enlightenment' occurs) that which was your individualization into the ego personality dissolves, so to speak... So from then on you are non-separate from existence...You do not experience anything as being separate from that point...YOU ARE THAT...When desire drops it is only karma that you continue to play out...but you are not involved within the action of the body...it is consciousness that moves you...

120. When the mind is stilled how do you think?

G: When someone asks a question the answer is just there...it appears within the framework of consciousness...There is no rational thought pattern that is happening...otherwise, since there is no longer any search, there is only silence...Any random thoughts that may occur are only clouds with no substance and not really recognized...

121. How can my relationship be used along the path?

G: Relationships are always good to work on the ego self.. It really puts ego out in your face so to speak... The more you can give in and not argue the point etc, the more you serve to break down the ego of the all important "i" verses the "I" of soul; which encompasses all beings equally...Only in breaking the "i" of self-importance do we progress...until we can once again drop the "i" for the "I" and become once again the ocean, instead of the drop...which in its self-appointed aloneness seeks to claim its importance...Only in non-importance does the important emerge...in all its glory...

122. What is Ego?

My dear seeker - Ego is that which you perceive yourself to be...such as body, emotions, thoughts, etc...You are living your illusions of truth through the conditions and conditionings of life...Enlightenment or Realization occurs when you drop all those illusions...When there are no longer any notions or ideations that 'I am this' or 'that'...when you go beyond the transient world and see the Eternal Formless Constant...That which holds all yet grasps nothing...When you rest within the Constant only then will you truly understand the transient world of Maya...Then you will KNOW that this is just a waking Dream State...And there is no bondage nor is there freedom for these are states that are created by mind alone...Enlightenment or Realization is when you go beyond mind and rationalizations, etc, etc. when you reach the Heart and the Essence of Being...For ONLY then do you truly live the life of unbound Bliss and Truth and Awareness which is Consciousness beyond mind...

123. What is Mouna (Silence) and Meditation?

G: True meditation is when there are no longer any thoughts...only the silence of awareness...no judgments, no rationalizing, nothing but Pure Awareness...otherwise it is not meditation but focused contemplation.

124. What about Fears?

G: It is the fear that you yourself generate and perceive as an illusion of truth, which is keeping you bound... as in Truth you have Never been bound...You exist in complete FREEDOM... But you create and sustain your illusions of truth such as: "I am not good enough"..."what if I fail"..."I am a failure for I have failed before"...All of these and I repeat, All of these are ego-generated fears alone...They have no truth, no validity...You alone keep yourself bound...it is your false perception of ego -

that you are that body and personality - which keeps you in this cycle of fear-induced perplexity...You are not the bound form... You the Self is the One that is Aware of the form...But it is not the form... the form only gives the medium of experience...But you are NOT the form...you are in Truth the Formless Constant which is of Eternal Existence...You are the ever vigilant Consciousness of Awareness...The bodies come and go as they will...Experience comes and goes as it will...The nature of things come and go...They are good, they are bad...Emotions are happy then they are sad... This IS the transient world...Constant Change...That is Nature...That is natural...But you are BEYOND ALL of the transient...The transient is your world of play and re-creation...And if you appear to make a wrong decision or fail, SO WHAT! Look at it again... Have you EVER truly failed at anything? NO! NEVER! ALL is a learning and wisdom-gaining experience...ALL...There are no right nor wrong choices... Life is just Life...it is here for direct experiential play to Discover the Truth of your Being...So relax......Go out and enjoy the play (as in a movie) and play (as in re-creation) of life...The *this* is the Maya Realm of Play and Experience...

The Pathless Zen - Simplified – Tools To Reveal The Truth

There is what you could call 'a path of no path' or sometimes I call it 'the simplified Zen Living'. This helps to center and to move you forward...every moment can be used for spiritual Sadhana...it must become a mindset...a natural way of Life...there are some techniques that you can use...it takes moving forward one step at a time...these are tools that I have found along the way...if you haven't started this practice then begin...so we have to:

1. Relax, just be aware of your breathing...go into the breath and completely relax...don't attempt to slow it, just be aware of it and then be aware of the body within centered in the heart... (right side of the chest)

2. Focus on ONE experience - one thing at a time (mindfulness)

3. Stay in the present (no past - no future)

4. Watch the thoughts and be aware of the body and space (active vipassana/witnessing)

5. Reject everything that you hold to be 'you' that is transient in nature until you come to what remains... the Essence. (Neti Neti)(Self-Enquiry)

6. Live your highest Truth at ALL times, honestly and ethically

7. See every moment as sacred and conduct yourself as such

8. Repeat the mantra OM... first be aware of the sound, the vibration and then switch and be aware of the silence...

9. Repeat an audible mantra - one which is very good is "I AM that I AM"

10. Repeat an open eye mantra while walking - "OM That I Am"... no matter what you see, say: "OM That I Am". (This breaks down your feeling of separation from existence and life)

11. Realize that every experience is transient in nature and that it will change

12. See rising emotions as simply movements of energized perception and don't label them.

13. Realize that energy is neutral - it is only our perception that makes it appear positive or negative.

14. Everything within the transient realm is directed and held in place by mind and the identity with your story experiences, when mind is transcended so are the illusions...

How To Use The Tools
Part 1

1. **Relaxing, just being aware of your breathing...**
Go into the breath and completely relax...Don't attempt to slow it, just be aware of it. It will slow and relax on its own. Eventually you will feel it come from the Hara point or diaphragm area.

What this one exercise can do for you is to center, ground, and give you the basis to be able to let go of what is coming up. This is the first and most important thing that may be taught. Don't let your focus be on anything except the breath. This may be done anywhere and anytime. Check it throughout the day. Anytime you feel a tension or tightening up then once again stop and go back into the relaxed breathing to once again gain stabilization.

Please do only this one exercise for at least one week before going onto to anything else.

2. **Focusing on one experience - Mindfulness**
Within this exercise one keeps one's mind and attention only upon the action at hand. Do not allow the mind to wander here and there. If there is walking then simply walk and be 100% aware and mindful of that activity alone. Do not think about what needs to be an hour from now or any other rising phenomena. Simply be aware of the walking or the looking at a flower and taking in its fragrance. In washing a plate simply wash the plate. Keep in mind the Zen Tea Ceremony in which simply preparing and drinking a cup of tea becomes a meditational exercise. You may turn any activity into a meditational, mindful awareness in motion. This will also help to slow the thoughts from wandering.

All of these exercises are here to help one see through the rising phenomena; to be able, instead of getting caught up in it

114

continually, to find a way to dispel it through seeing the inherent nature behind it.

3. Staying in the present. (No past - no future).
Life may only be lived in the Present.

4. Watching the thoughts and being aware of the body and space. (Vipassana or witnessing)
First sit and simply become aware of the breath. Then start to extend the attention to the feelings that arise within the body form. As they come up let them go and do not cling to any of them. You can start there and then slowly extend the attention to more subtle awareness of the mind.

See the thoughts but do not gravitate to them. Do not chase after them. Simply watch them as a progressing show like some foreign film. Soon you will see rising patterns and when you are distanced enough, the next part comes into play.

5. Rejecting everything that you hold to be 'you'
Reject all that is transient in nature - until you come to what remains - the Essence or Source. (Neti-Neti or Self-Enquiry)

In this, you begin to question, "where does the 'I' arise from? What is it? What holds it in place?" As Krishnamurti said, enquire into it "deeply". Go to the very heart of it. Or you may question by the process of 'not this' and 'not this'. Is the physical body constant in nature? If it is not, then it cannot be the unchanging Source? So it would be Neti-Neti or 'not this'... Go into the emotions and mind. Where do they rise from and go to? This is not an intellectual exercise, but one that takes time and a settled and relaxed looking and contemplating to its very depths.

When the ego self that keeps the conditionings in place goes, then Self-Realization is entered and the kundalini completes in that moment. This was also the finding of Sri Ramana Maharshi; that Self-Enquiry brings the kundalini back to the central or Satvik and neutral - balanced position. The process of Self-Enquiry will bring the kundalini to a natural and safe completion. Know also that all phenomena is in motion and cannot be the Unchanging Source.

Therefore, for now, let it go.

6. Living you highest Truth at all times, honestly and ethically.

If you always live what you know to be true and do everything in an honest and ethical way then nothing can ever come back to disturb your mind or consciousness.

How To Use The Tools
Part 2

7. Seeing every moment as Sacred and conducting yourself as such.

In each moment is the Divine in motion. See all of life as sacred and it will become so. This develops the mind of Bhakti or Love, and this once again brings a love for all life and opens the heart to see with the eyes of the divine.

8. Repeating the mantra OM.

First be aware of the sound and the vibration then switch and become aware of the silence it rests within and proceeds from...This brings one into the moment. This also can keep one moving towards a stilled mind and also the awareness of silence.

9. Repeating the audible mantra "I AM That I AM" (closed eyes).

This mantra has an excellent centering and also vibrational pattern. It can help to relax one and to once again help to still the mind.

10. Repeating the open eye mantra - "OM THAT I AM"

This mantra can help your realize your oneness with all things. It breaks down your feeling of separation from existence and life in general. This may be repeated audibly or silently.

11. Realizing that every experience is transient in nature and that it will indeed change.

No matter what comes see that it will indeed change. All things within the transient realm are in the midst of fluctuation and change. It is all fluid in nature. So no matter how great or how devastating something seems in the moment, realize that it cannot be clung to. Indeed it Will change. And nothing has any more power over you than you yourself accept.

12. Seeing rising emotions as simply movements of energized perception - not labeling them.

No matter what emotion arises, don't give it a name and thereby own it. If one simply steps back and goes into the relaxed breathing and sees it and feels it as a moving energy, it diffuses quite rapidly. It is no longer fear or anger, but simply a burst of adrenaline and a rush of feeling through the physical form. If you can let it go without naming it, it simply becomes another fluid movement that rises from the ocean in a wave and then once again returns to the same ocean. Step back and watch the phenomenal nature of it.

13. Realizing that energy is neutral. It is only our perception that makes it appear positive or negative.

Energy has no positive or negativity within itself. It is simply the primal substance in movement. Mind creates the division of positive and negative. So no matter what energy rises within you, or what you feel and are aware of, know that it has no power of positive or negative. When no attention is given then all energy will fade. Attention feeds it. Attention moves it. The best thing to do in the case of an overabundance of kundalini blockage is not to attempt to push the energy but to divert the attention to stilling and thereby diffusing it.

14. Everything within the transient realm is directed and held in place by mind and the identity with your story experiences, when the mind is transcended so are the illusions.

This is very important. All the conditionings are simply mind and ego self accepted bondages. Conditionings, name, etc. keep the ego form in place. When the illusive and empty nature is seen and known it will dissipate. Self-Enquiry will take you face to face with identity and conditionings... Kundalini puts everything in your face to see through as the empty illusion that it is. Once that is done then it has no more hold. The mind/body will become clear and the cellular memory will be at an end as well. What will remain is a new being that KNOWS the transient and Eternal as ONE.

Please do not rush through these exercises as they are life-changing patterns that should be put into place one by one as living Sadhana or as a living spiritual endeavor. You will notice as you go into each of these that perceptions will begin to change. Life may become less solid and more fluid. Have no fear, it will in the end, balance out to become quite whole. When the notion of individual self has been lost in the Ocean of One then the kundalini will have reached its completion. The path may be at an end and the searching over, but you will find that LIFE is just beginning in this present moment. Recognize that the past is the past. It cannot be changed. The only way the future changes, is by living well in this moment. So all in all this is the moment which matters. You may only truly live in the now - otherwise you only exist.

Begin to watch the mind and when it starts delving into the past - Stop - and come back to now. If need be do something physical to divert the attention back to the moment of now. Or one may do a mantra to bring one back to the now or the relaxed breathing, which also can center and still one. Use any of the above tools to bring you back into the present moment of now.

Sages Celebrate...

S: In all persons, places, things and events there is great bliss. That is our true nature. When we engage our minds in the internal dialogue of splitting the underlying unity of all things into subject/object sentences...even to read this communication...unless we have become accustomed to residing in that ground of all being, which is ONE without Second, the bliss is reduced or lost altogether.

G: Unless the divisionary realm contains great love and celebration of ALL aspects of the divine this indeed may become the case...when tied up in the "I" and "MY" story, the celebration of others as self receeds greatly... Let us see and celebrate the diversity of the ONE...Bliss is found within and not in circumstances...when the ONE is known it IS the whole of existence and we are THAT...so I agree swami-ji - a grand celebration is in order...

S: That is why the great saints and sages, both past and present, have recommended meditation. That dip into the ONENESS continually reminds us of our true nature. It shows us the way home again. And as the path home becomes more and more defined by use, we can visit that place more often and stay longer.

G: Once entered into wholly it may remain undisturbed...until that moment there are glimpses and forays within that HOLY Place...but the great secret is that the HOLY PLACE is always Right Here...Right Now...just let go of the separation and need to *find* it...it is Here...it is everywhere - equally – undivided...what keeps it at bay is simply our belief that it is Here within any moment if only we let down all of our guards and reservations...when they are stripped away one simply falls into this Holy Presence...When living from that awareness there is no longer the; looking at who is living from there... the 'who' receeds... there is simply This Moment and it is Bliss as it IS...there is simply Creation that is the body of God in Motion...What an adventure...

S: When you arrive at that hOMe, the subject/object dichotomy is a useful tool; but it is not mistaken for the ultimate reality. Words, symbols, rational thought are maps. They are not the territory. Maps are useful things. Don't discard your maps....just reside in your hOMe.

G: All comes from the OM - OM permeates and maintains existence...OM resides within the Ever Present Silence of Source...Source IS and OM proceeds movement into form...All is vibrational Bliss within the transient realm...A symphony that plays its eternal tune... Source is infinite possiblity...Om is the play of possibility into actualization...or the reflection of Mind into a viable form of cognition...the Original Mind is free of all conditioned babble and simply rests within the simplicity of now...no dark colorizations...simply the Bliss of Pure Awareness of the ONE beyond distinction and yet reveling within the play of distinctions...

...The Power of the Mantra
(Western Contemplative)

Thank you God, for the opportunity to be here and to experience this life.

J: Now there's a powerful 'mantra'. Gratitude for this life and every breath is an expression of Grace. To even have this thought come to mind and feel what it means to you comes from a beautiful place inside that is drawing you near.

G: Gratitude is a big step along the way...the savoring of life and every minute is indeed Grace...the joyous bounty of existence...

J: By keeping this thought, and then allowing the words to dissolve after a time, without losing the 'glow' they have produced, we are able to move into our experience as only consciousness.

G: Words are Creation... *The word was with God and the word Was God...* Word is that which creates and sustains the mindset and perception...Word is very important within the transient realm...Source is beyond spoken word within the Silence ever present...When there are no words left to speak...when the breath catches in awe and wonder...in that moment is a doorway to the eternal One...

J: It is here, in the silent being of consciousness that the door may open to full-blown Realization, remembrance and understanding. In this way we move beyond the focusing purpose of the mantra to the feelings provoked by the expression of gratitude, then to a perfect point of silence from which comes perfect peace of mind.

G: Every word is a mantra...every sound projected is a living mantra of creative wonder... what does your creation hold?

J: "To those who fix their mind on God, He will grant perfect peace of mind."

G: The stilled mind sees only Peace and gentle Knowing...

J: Many Westerners have been taught to use a Hindu, or unintelligible word as a mantra to focus their attention and quiet the internal dialogue. And that's fine. But this approach; using a phrase as a mantra that evokes powerful feelings and stirs positive emotions, I feel, is a very powerful way to move toward (or back to) our natural Enlightenment.

G: Yes when entered into fully...anything which moves one may be used as a mantra...

J: "Enter His gates with thanksgiving"

G: And Sing His Glory with Praises... isn't that what it is all about...? finding the realm of Heaven that is at hand...be willing to let go of hell so that Heaven may be Entered...

(Eastern Guru Mantra)

S: The mysteries of mantra are great indeed. I agree with you that after a certain point in sadhana everything becomes a mantra... especially the internal unstruck sound of nada...Great Bliss.

G: Yes there is a point wherein the vibrational purity of sound may take one ever further inwards until all is dispelled...the sound of OM may be felt to reverberate in and through sound...coming from and resting within the Pregnant Eternal Void which is beyond yet penetrates and encompasses all of creation...

S: At the beginning and up until one is roaming in the infinity of the Heart Chakra, the Guru Mantra is really necessary for the Sadhaka. This is where a live Guru...an incarnation if you will...is so necessary. Feelings of gratitude...in fact any feeling at all...can be a diversion to Realization Gratitude, like its cousin Compassion, is best realized at the higher stages of Awareness.

G: Indeed this is why a living Mantra is given...I indeed will give a mantra as such to students...A mantra which is uttered by the Realized sage and is given to their devotees or Sadhakas does carry some transmission seed if done from the Heart in full awareness...

S: The Guru Mantra...there are more than 80,000 of them...is given by the Guru to the Sadhaka. It is infused with a Shakti (a power, a force, an energy, an expression of the Non-Dual) that no other Mantra derived from reading or intuiting by the Sadhaka can equal. It is the Grace Bestowing Power of God..."and the word was God." It does not indicate that any word was/is God (until after a certain state is realized).

G: There is a time when you reach a certain point wherein ALL words are done as mantram...until that time is entered...until the time of the purity of word through Nad and wisdom is entered... then indeed an infused Mantra is appropriate...this mantra works as long as done from the Heart in total awareness, sincerity, and with continued connection with the Guru that has given and infused this mantra...to this, I agree...

S: Natural Enlightenment is only viable for the Sadhaka after he/she abides in the state of Realization. Yes! That state is our natural state...anything else is illusion. Realization of that which is ONE WITHOUT SECOND is the TRUTH.

G: Yes, all have, at the core of Being, Original Mind...that which is ever clear and undisturbed...but it becomes clouded over with the heavy conditionings of misplaced and misbegotten mindsets...

S: It has been my experience that at many plateaus I have taken it to be the final destination. It even happened to Buddha. It takes a GURU to verify the state of Grace. In all those plateaus though, I had some doubts...at the end...which is the beginning ...OM...there are no doubts.

G: Yes, I feel this is the way with all of us...many times along the journey I felt that there was Enlightenment...but there was still no internal peace...so delusion remained and was only fooling myself...It took my Guru to break through the illusion of wisdom... hahahaha...and in the end it was the Guru that indeed validated when true Enlightenment was entered...for it is as you say... There is no conviction...for within conviction lie the seeds of doubt...within Self-Realization and Non-Dual Vijnana there is NO Doubt...it is Unshakable...Unflappable Reality...This does not change... it is unending Grace...simply the gentle Peace which passes understanding remains...No matter what life brings it is there...along with the undercurrent of Bliss...

THE DISSOLUTION OF SELF AND KUNDALINI

*** My former teacher in Magick told me that to overcome all the kundalini problems it would require the 'Total Dissolution of Self'. (Crowley wrote something along that line in the Liber Al). He interprets this as the dissolution of the Self image, and says, it is the Self image that has to be recreated from that point onwards.

G: It is not recreated it is the baggage that goes... it is only when one has entered into Self-Realization that the process ends...that is what is termed 'merging Shiva into Shakti'. It takes going beyond the mundane transient and into the Source or Heart of Existence...that takes going beyond mind and the relative ways and means of knowledge and knowing...once that is done through Self-Enquiry and entering into the death before death then indeed, the self image simply dissolves into the Source....

*** With Self-Realization you mean that which remains, when the past and the future, the active workings of the mind and the 'relative ways and means of knowledge and knowing' are stripped away? So that the term 'self image' becomes meaningless, because all but the core is irrelevant?

G: There is NO self 'Image' that remains...in the moment of Realization or being pulled into Source there is no world seen... there is no 'I' that remains as such...there is only that which has been from time immemorial...it is like total Intellect but without 'relative knowledge'...you KNOW this is IT...there is nothing in the Universe which is NOT This...and yet it has No personal sense...No Face...What remains after that experience is simply a moving integration within the totality of the universe...once that is done through Self-Enquiry and entering into the death before death then indeed the self image simply dissolves into the Source...

*** With "death before death" do you mean the state where the body is as if dead, very cold, almost not breathing, because the kundalini has taken so much of yourself out of the body?

G: They say the body indeed gets cold but in that moment unless someone else is around to see there is no cognition of it...there is no cognition of the transient world at all... no connection with form, emotion or identity. There is simply a KNOWING of the 0...Simply in that moment ONLY the Formless Constant. Only the Primordial Pregnant Void IS...and you are THAT...there is no thought in that time...only when coming back into some movement of mind is that which has transpired Known through the avenue of attempting to put it in a framework of relatives... it is beyond mind and duality and so there is no language that is possible to adequately describe the moment of Self-Realization...and within that moment your whole world and paradigm is forever altered...the transient world then becomes fully empty in nature from that moment onwards...you become fully human... there is no false humility as it is KNOWN that ALL seen and unseen is simply the Source... there is no more attempting to 'build' or 'sustain' a self...there is the limitational form which is there for experiential knowing and relationship...what is ever related to is within the Self... that is all...

*** *I think he [Crowley] talks much, when the day is long, but since the possibility that he is right is a non-negligible possibility, I would like to hear some other POVs on how this 'Dissolution of Self' could otherwise be interpreted.*

G: There is no other interpretation except that the self must die first for the Source to be Known...

*** *I understand. Does this happen by itself when you enter the "death before death"? You must know, that I think my mate is very close now, and I have the feeling, that there is just a little thing that remains to solve itself, like a button opening up. Probably something he doesn't want to let go completely.*

G: Yes...It stays as long as one does not come back and then once again attempt to rebuild an ego self...The last step is total surrender...in attempting to hold onto a shred one will not complete... There may be glimpses and insights but no merging...Kundalini ends when the transient is merged within the Constant...when ego is merged and lost within the

Divine...When relative is immersed and lost within the Unknowable Purity of Forever Undiminished Source...

*** *I once read something, that the memory losses that can be symptoms of kundalini could have something to do with it, as if a 'separation' of one's own past, with all the problems rooted within that past, is necessary. A consequence of this could be a different 'energy signature' ('frequency signature').*

G: Memory losses do occur... nothing to stress about... it will all adjust...what needs to remain will remain...what doesn't simply goes...but time losses also may occur along the way...don't worry about energy signatures...everything within the transient universe is composed of moving and vibrating energy...it is constantly in flux...you are what you are.

*** *I dreamed last night, that one who has achieved the dissolution of self is able to stand on a slippery soap stone (which was round, and impossible to stand on) I thought it referred to making the now eternal (the moment you step on the stone) Can you make sense of this?*

G:.hahahahahaha...yes...this signifies that whatever is impossible to do within the transient may only be accomplished within the Formless Constant of Self Recognition...not of a created identity...but that which is the Core of ALL Existence...once that is KNOWN the world is empty in nature...there is simply the Peace that remains...it is always remaining in infinite possibility...What holds - creates - sustains and moves the world is the MIND...Mind moves the energy into patterns... the patterns form creation...Spoken words are Vibrational Patterns... these set the universe in motion...there is nothing impossible when source is KNOWN...

SATSANG

WHAT RELIGION ARE YOU?

If people ask me if I am Hindu or Christian etc...I simply say I am all and none...I am the Truth which is contained within all religions and yet which is not bound by any...I am the unbound Truth which all rests within... drop the dogma of man and ego and you will find the pure Truth of Existence...All these I AM...and yet am not for the dogma and outward appearances are all transients which come and go and I AM the Constant Source Which cannot be contained or held by any church or doctrine or religion...I AM the Simplicity of Reality...Nature seen and Spirit unseen... One beyond the forms which contains all forms yet which is separate and distinct within the Self...All Reflection of this world comes from the Supreme Self Alone... Go beyond the Reflection to the Formless Self of knowledge, bliss and conscious awareness of the ever pure Spirit...the Holy Spirit of Truth made Manifest...Manifesting I Am the Reality behind All of Existence...The ever pure untainted Spirit of Truth...All is from this Truth... YOU are this Truth...Let go of the false notions of ego centered personality and BE THE TRUTH THAT YOU ARE!

THE FORMLESS CONSTANT

What is God but the Formless Constant?
What is man but the transient ego?
Drop your name and identity with the world of duality and what and who are you then?
Do you cease to exist? Or do you exist completely?!
Or does your existence lie only within the framework of the body?
The elements of the body come from earth and return to earth...
WAKE UP! YOU ARE THE FORMLESS--THAT WHICH IS--BEYOND TIME AND BEYOND CONSTRAINTS...
YOU ARE THAT...SAT-CHIT-ANAND...that draws around itself the veil of Maya and ignorance of self (ego) and ignorance

of 'Self' (the constant Source) to engage in the dream of the transient.. .the ego exists only as a dream for ALONE I AM THE SUPREME SELF OF EXISTENCE...

THE MOMENT OF NOW

In reading these words you must reflect, and in reflecting you have missed the Now...
for the Now is not of mind and thought and reflection...
The Now is only found and maintained while in pure awareness...
Direct awareness not reflection...
In reflection there is subject and object
and in pure awareness the division is absent...
Neither can you say that you perceive or experience for this also is subjective and objective…
The Now is not a state for states are of mind…
If you can speak of it then again it becomes reflection
and you are in the past…
The Now cannot be gauged by time for it is Constant
yet ever-flowing in the Maya realm…
The Emptiness holds Nothing yet All Manifests within it...
Devoid of substance like a dream, the Maya realm of mind comes and goes.
Ever empty in nature...And the Now beyond mind is Constant in nature
While the Maya realm of mind and thought is ever in flux…
And within the Emptiness of Now they are both non-dual in nature...

THE DREAM

Another day has come and gone...
another dream unfolds
overlapping one to another.
we forage through to the truth beyond...
Let me not be so caught up in the dream of the transient
that the Constant is not lived...

For truly the Constant is the Ultimate truth....

and the rest is icing on the cake...
The emptiness which proceeds from Consciousness as form...
The dreams of life that are held so dear...
and yet we are IT ALL and yet beyond it All...
the Emptiness of Formless Consciousness...
Rest in the Silence of Bliss, Consciousness and Truth...
Sat-Chit-Anand...

KNOWLEDGE AND OBSERVATION

Reading is a good way to begin...but intellectual knowledge is not true understanding...
Only in the 'direct' experience can you truly understand and KNOW... before then it is only once again hearsay....

These writings are put forth so that you have a path or a guide...to prove or disprove...to those that agree then I say go into the silence and find out for sure it is truth...and to those that disagree I say then go into the silence and prove me wrong...this is all...nothing more and nothing less...(the silence is found in the merging of Shiva and Shakti or the transient within the Constant.)

To start your path, observe...and step back....Observe and step back...this is a first step...
Be the action and do not judge it or think of it... Just BE...
Just observe...without restrictions...

To fully enter the silence then let us develop first focused awareness and detachment...and the mind will slow its extraneous thoughts...and it is much easier to drop a single idea than a multitude of circling thoughts and ideations...Become simplicity itself... Simplify... slow down... observe...detach...and Be...

GOD?

God only exists with aspects through the Maya realm of this world...

Beyond this world that which is called God has no such aspects nor any division...

God is beyond any division...and all that is seen as creation is only a division of God... God is ALL that exists... God is that spark of light which is life itself...

It is only the mind of man which creates division and sees not the Truth...

This world is here for God to play and for us to realize we are not this ego form of body which comes and goes...

We are spirit in essence which is eternal... and all in this world is of the flesh which comes and goes...

Nothing in the Maya realm is eternal, it all is in constant flux and change...

Realization is seeing this world for what it is and knowing the Eternal Changeless Formless which holds the Maya realm, yet which is beyond and is not touched by it...

Do not despair, this is the realm of experience... But we are beyond all such experience...

When you drop the ego of division All that exists is God...

See beyond the limited form of ego and dogma in all its forms...

TANTRIC MISCONCEPTIONS

In the West they take the name of Tantra to sell sex... *Gee whiz, guilt-free sex, and I can say I'm spiritual at the same time... What a deal!*

While Tantra can use all things to progress on the path, the sexual aspects are very misunderstood...

True Tantra is all about breaking the existing conditions and conditionings within your life... It is about dropping ego and doership instead of promoting more... You need to come to the place of no body consciousness... you transcend and become One with the universe...

There is no separation between you and existence or your partner etc...

Unfortunately they use orgasm as a substitute for the Bliss or Anand that is spoken of in scripture...This Anand is reached only within yourself...It is not reached by having a partner...

The right hand path seeks to integrate the Self and there is no sex involved... The left hand path does include sex...But if it is seen as sex then that is what it is... The left hand path is a two-edged sword...You must be at the point of contemplative meditation where you ARE your partner... Before this, it only creates more ego sense of 'I am this body and this personality'...This is the danger of the sexual usage...But if you are at the end of the path and you can totally merge within the Being of your partner then in reality you don't need that path any longer anyway...

ALIVE

Being Alive in every moment...
Utterly and completely Alive!!!
There is no death for me, for I AM the Formless Constant which holds ALL and
Pervades All...
Beyond the transitory I AM...
Time and fragmentation of Spirit into the bound form of ego, is not...
For I AM FREE beyond constraints and conditions...
I AM the boundless Bliss of Being!!
Forever situated within the Supreme Self Alone...

FINALLY THE SELF APPEARS

No more entertaining the mind of thoughts.
Nor dreaming the dream of death...
For finally the Self appears! the non-self is no more;
vanishing as dew upon a hot day.
And when the ego self is slain in that moment beyond time...
what is there that remains?
Consciousness walking in Bliss...
Awakened to the Truth of Emptiness...

The Formless Constant Beyond Aspects...and Maya becomes the playground of dream...The transient thought-created realm of self-imposed limitations of experience...
And All exists in Bliss!!

GUIDED CONTEMPLATION

Let your breathing naturally slow and let a good two breaths come between each concept and line... Explore and Be each concept and TRUTH as it unfolds... you may either read or record and listen back... BUT IT IS ESSENTIAL THAT MINIMUM TWO BREATHS OF SPACE ARE GIVEN... There must be time for each Truth to sink in and be explored and manifested within your reality framework...

THE CONTEMPLATION of SELF

Lying here I AM the earth... (2 slow breaths)
The elements of earth comprise my body... (2)
Let them return to the earth.... (2)
My veins are the Ganges river, flowing Pure... (2)
It is said if you bathe once in the Ganga you will gain liberation.... (2)
I AM the Ganga... (2)
My breath is the breeze that pushes the clouds across the sky... (2)
I AM the winds that blow here and there... (2)
One eye is the Sun... (2)
The other the Moon... (2)
My head contains the sky, pure and expansive...(2)
My thoughts are the stars... (2)
Pinpoints of LIGHT made Manifest... (2)
My words are the OM... (2)
The VIBRATION of OM... (2)
I Am the OM the fabric of the universe... (2)
Going beyond I AM the ZERO... (2)
The void from which ALL EMERGES... (2)
Self Contained... (2)
Complete within the SELF of GOD... (2)

From here I Breath the worlds into EXISTENCE... (2)
OM SOHAM BRAHMAN... (2)
OM SOHAM BRAHMAN... (2)
OM SOHAM BRAHMAN... (2)
I AM the LIVING BREATHING MANTRA of OM... (2)
OM SOHAM... (2)
OM SOHAM... (2)
I AM the SILENCE of the EVER-PRESENT NOW... (2)
Which EXTENDS into ETERNITY... (2)
Beyond time... (2)
Beyond constraints... (2)
I AM ONE WITH THE SUPREME SELF... (2)
I AM ONE WITH THE SUPREME SELF, THE HEART OF
BLISS, THAT RADIATES
THROUGHOUT THE UNIVERSE AS ONE... (2)
I AM ONE WITH THAT SUPREME SELF... (2)
I AM GANESH the dispeller of obstacles... (2)
I AM SHIVA Consciousness Itself... (2)
I AM SHAKTI Energy, Power, Kundalini Manifest... (2)
I AM RADHA devotion complete... (2)
I AM KRISHNA infinite love... (2)
I AM BUDDHA one with compassion... (2)
I AM YESHUA the TRUTH MADE MANIFEST... (2)
I AM TARA everlasting enlightenment... (2)
I AM THE WORD OM MADE FLESH...YET BEYOND
THE FLESH I AM... (2)
PURE VIBRATORY BLISS I AM... (2)
SAT-CHIT-ANAND
TRUTH OF REALITY...AWARENESS...AND BLISS
I AM...(2)
HARI OM TAT SAT ... I AM THAT TRUTH... THE
VIBRATORY BLISS OF OM... (2)
THE CONSTANT MANTRA OF SOHAM AM I... (2)
ONE WITH THE SUPREME SELF OF
EXISTENCE I AM... (2)
OM SOHAM... (2)
OM SOHAM... (2)
OM SOHAM... (2)
I HAVE ENTERED THE PEACE WHICH PASSES ALL
UNDERSTANDING... (2)
THE ETERNAL LIVING WATERS I AM... (2)

THE CONSTANT SILENCE OF AWARENESS I AM... (2)
OM... (2)
AMEN... (2)
I AM THAT I AM... (2)
SAT-CHIT-ANAND... (2)
HARI OM TAT SAT... (2)
THE CONSTANT NOW OF AWARENESS I AM... (2)
THE SILENT NOW OF AWARENESS I AM... (2)
AWARENESS I AM... (2)
OM... THE WORD OF GOD.... OM... (2)

This is a long but fruitful contemplation...enjoy the journey to discover the center of your Being... the Supreme Self...

Love and Blessings from the world of Shakti...BE A GREAT EXISTENCE!!

PERFECTION

PERFECTION
Hum! The dreaded 'perfection' trap...go out into nature and look at a tree or a mountain....is it symmetrical? With handmade pottery sometimes it is the imperfections that make it perfect...it is perfect no matter what!! So relax and let yourself go...look at the modern art...is it perfect in design? What is perfection to one is someone else's nightmare...

Perfection is objective...Go with the flow...relax and enjoy...if it is stressful then you are 'trying' too hard...in your 'trying' for perfection you are defeated...so just be the observer and be 'amazed' at what occurs and comes out of your relaxed creativity... and know that no matter what comes out it is 'perfect' as it is...

JUDGING

You are right in that you cannot judge another's space...
each is based in their 'own' reality...
What is relaxing to one is mind-jarring to another...
What is your truth is not another's view of truth.
That is why you only find liberation within the Self...
You come in alone…

and you go out alone...
All of your emotions and thoughts are yours alone...
Although all are from and contain the same Self - the ego form
and mindset is a never-ending maze of difference...
Only in Realization does all this end when the One Truth
brings all the paradoxes in line...
All are living within their own version of reality...
You are only responsible for your actions and re-actions...
and you are not responsible for anyone else's...
you can only change your own view of the world
not anyone else's.
We want to be able to fix everyone...
but they have a right to their misery if that is what they wish...
and sometimes mercy is when someone falls very hard and very
fast...
sometimes the shock of the fall will wake them up to the fact
that there is more than the transient realm of existence...
so see, and observe, but judge nothing...
All are moving with the nature of their self...
towards discovery of the 'Self'...
and it is all perfect and in balance no matter what the outer
appearances are...

WHY THE SILENCE - WHY NOT MIND
(NOT TWO - CREATION / UNCREATED IS)

There is a quote: "*Those that speak do not know and those that
know do not speak.*"
There are those that have reached that have tried to speak...
but always say there are no adequate words...
You cannot describe That Which Is or the Constant or God
beyond Form or the Source...it is impossible...many have tried
but it becomes a lesson in futility...through trying the great
works such as the *Viveka-chudamani* and the *Ashtavakra Gita*
came into being...
Now the answer as to why it is impossible...
Because the Word is thought...and word and thought are
creation... and creation is duality... All words denote form...

even those that state 'formless' just give another quality to form... Mind and thought create the Maya realm of form and the transient...

That Which Is the Constant is beyond all division and duality and form...So when you speak, Maya comes into existence...

The moment you speak you are separate from That Which Is...

So now how to reach...

That is *why* the Silence...inner silence...why emotions and mind and thought must stop...only then will you go beyond the intellect...only then can you reach the unreachable...only in the silence...when mind and thought stop...then you go beyond to that which Is...then you go beyond the transient to the Constant...

In silence the world of Maya ends... in non-thought then true knowledge IS... in Pure Awareness that which is Reality Is... To reach you must be willing to drop the world of the transient that you have held so dear...

The fear that you cease to exist is unfounded...for you will find that while that which is seen as personality ends...you are One in the lap of reality...

You are what the transient world proceeds from...You are the Essence of Existence and beyond Existence...

Then if you desire personality and form go for it...for you will find you are and have always been free...this is Moksha... to finally understand that there is Nothing that you need freedom from...that it was and is All only a play of mind in the ever-changing transient realms...realms of desire and experience...

The dream state of Maya...

Realization is beyond experience...although experience is the closest word of duality to explain Being in That...

Experience has a beginning and an end...and Truth has no beginning nor end...

Self has never been born nor has ever died...although it sustains and gives life and meaning to form, the experience of form does not touch it...

You are the perfection untouched by any experience of form and Maya...

Just as you are untouched by your dreams at night...the You of Self is untouched by the Maya realm of dream and mind...

Go within to the Silence...drop the thought...just observe...

Have no preconceptions... Just BE!

TO INTELLECTUALS WHO DISPUTE ADVAITA

While Krishnamurti is wonderful, unless you know beyond a shadow of a doubt through direct experience that of which he speaks, then it only becomes a futile, intellectual battle built on hearsay - and what you think may 'perhaps' be true...What Krishnamurti has spoken of and what I speak of is what is KNOWN from direct knowledge...and it only comes when you go beyond mind and thought... for any thought or word brings concepts and form into being... and then you are separate into the world of Maya...This is why it is impossible to explain fully...for any word that I would try to use sets up limitations and boundaries, and concepts...even if I say "formless", it only brings to mind a state or quality of form...

While intellect can discard one thing at a time as transient and therefore not the Constant or Source...it cannot take you to the ultimate Truth of Existence beyond existence or the Maya realm from which it has proceeded... there must in the end come a total surrender and letting go to enter and be dissolved into Source... but perhaps you do not wish to hear this from me now and that is fine too...you are entitled to your view of truth or your illusion of truth, whatever it is...

The Emptiness which holds the All is not a void of flatness but pregnant with all that is or will be...It is the potential for that which is expressed in form...All I can say is that in going beyond mind and thought in the silence you will find that all you thought to be true drops in an instant...and you KNOW that the Maya realm is only a more extended dream state...it no longer has the hold on you... the illusions are dropped...and That Which Is or Source is All that remains...It is the Constant and permeates all but is untouched by any of the proceedings in the Maya realm of the transient... the Essence of your Being is only that Source...Beyond a shadow of a doubt you have never been born nor never died, the essence of you IS...Eternal...all that happens, happens only to form and to your mental illusions that you are only the body in this existence...but to the real you that is ever-eternal - Nothing can touch or harm nor change its eternal nature...which is Bliss, and the Emptiness that is Complete containing All in potentiality...no longer personal limitational form...it is more real than anything which you now view in the Maya realm...and this is Realization...simply to come to that place...where there is no within or without...it simply IS...and there are no longer any questions...nor any disputes…nor any conviction, for in conviction there must be doubt somewhere, and there is NO Doubt...the path ends...and liberation is won... for you find there has never been anything to be liberated from...and you see the Maya realm for what it is...a playground of mind and desire...the ever transient world in change...the only constant is change...And you see the emptiness in it and know it is non-dual in nature also...and you rest in the Silence beyond 'rational' mind and thought...no thoughts floating in endless succession...and if any arise they are only empty clouds that pass without any substance...

When the thoughts end - and even the desire for liberation and enlightenment has been dropped, then and only then does the shift take place...and All changes in a split second...The world is not and only the Substance...the Essence...the Truth beyond Division remains...you are no longer witness...for there must be subject and object to be witnessed... you are not a witness of anything...yet you are...Complete and Whole with more Life and Bliss than you can ever obtain in the transient fleeting world of Maya...Simply you are...and yet you are not...for there is no person...no body...no mind...no thought... no mentally sustained ideation of a 'you'...Yet you are Real and the Eternal Nature that gives life...sustains life...and is life...

As Ego Dissolves
The Letters

As Ego Dissolves 1

Dear Ganga,
Namaste Dear ONE

About six weeks ago things came to a particular kind of climax for me and something has changed in and for me since then. I would like to tell you about it and I was hoping you could give me some feedback.

I have written to you in the past and you have given me extremely good advice regarding my meditation, moving it from straight Vipassana to Neti-Neti. Whilst doing this I have continued with an intensive long term therapy with a very sensitive and open minded psychologist - I felt I needed the support. Neti-Neti however was the prime mover in shifting me to this experience. It cut so deep and opened me to total vulnerability. To cut a long story short I came to a profound impasse in my negotiation of misery and despair. I suddenly saw my construction of it and in seeing that I felt totally destroyed. It was like my mind gave way. I saw how the despair wasn't going anywhere and never would. I saw I wanted out, I wanted a cure, I wanted all of my past to not have been, none of which I now saw could possibly happen.

In that state I felt many of my illusions shattered, but in that something else happened. I felt something still deep in me. That space I have made contact with periodically with the practice of Neti-Neti but now it spilled over. I was so overcome that I fell asleep for a couple of hours even though it was only 10:30 in the morning.

On awakening, deep within me I felt so calm or rather totally emptied out of my sense of personal content. Terror and violent energy seemed to rage around me and yet I was completely untouched at a core level. I could just watch the show and it was spectacular. I felt I had no face, no shape. Things in the world and me seemed without name - they had shape but no content. I could feel/see large movements in the visible world. This feeling has not left me. Something seems irremediably changed.

I feel intense emotions as I always have but strangely seem untouched by them - almost as though they are happening to someone else. Indeed the strong feelings seem stimulated by these changes. It is like I am afraid and yet can't seem to feel it and this makes even more fear storms rage around me and yet nothing! I feel strong even when weak, and weak even when strong - I feel I don't feel. I know this sounds strange but this is what it is like. I feel that all these 'feelings' are my old states and my old states don't seem to like this shift!! It seems to me that as I continue just to watch them they will fall away - indeed it feels that is happening as I type. This all seems to have happened when I felt at my most helpless and lost. I was at the end of what I could do to change my life, nothing could or would ever work. I was always going to be who I was or rather who I am - if that doesn't sound too contradictory. Paradoxically nothing really has changed and yet I am not who I was. Who am I? I can't find me. I can see the effects of me but it doesn't feel like me. I feel like a big empty space. When I look into that it feels very sweet because there is no pain in there, no me, just smooth peace, so open so sweet, so free of me and if I stay there full - I can love so much from there. When I slow, find solitude and reach 'within' I feel an expanding clearness and I see beauty - no aloneness. It seems so final. I have never experienced anything like this, not for so long. I also am beginning to sleep blissfully.

I can't really think of much more to say that would add to this. Any comments?
Do you know what this might be?
In love,

Congratulations! You have found the core SELF... that Eternal Unchanging Formless Constant which is the Great Potential which comes into manifest form...What is happening is the patterns that were generated all of your life continue to play out until exhausted... that is all...there is no need to stress about it...simply remain within that Center where no 'personal you' is found...the personal story is wrapped up in forms'...identity...you are NOT nor ever have been the form... the form is simply a vehicle of Expression...

You are living within the NOW...It appears you reached the final confrontational seeing and then surrendered where indeed the whole shatters and the story is seen for what it is...Do not fear...as you stay within this Silence and Stilled Being the remaining play will fall away if you do not once again take back the external mind and form and divisionary experience as paramount...Simply remain as you are...The dream continues yet you are finally awakened to see the play for what it is...Congratulations...There is no need to recall or cling to name and the storyline...let them fall away as past...continue forward within the Peace and start to Live the Miracle of Life as it IS...

Love and Blessings Sat*Chit*Anand Shanti-Shanti-Shanti OM
.g.

As Ego Dissolves 2

Dear Ganga:
Namaste Dear One -

I'm continuing as usual tracking the self twenty-four hours a day. New experiences always arise, but nothing final yet.

Well am sure if the final comes you will write right away... hahahahahaha...

The consciousness has a sense of travel to it when I'm meditating. One night when I was awake laying in bed, I felt as if I was just consciousness traveling down a tunnel and lost touch with my body.

Good... just keep surrendering.

In a dream, one evening I felt as if I was being pulled into a black void.

Yes good there is still further to go...so keep surrendering...

I continue seeing religious visions during meditation, lights breaking through darkness, patterns and colors. All of them crystal clear. I still see a variety of colors around; blue, green, yellow and purple and always after a new intense experience, I see big blobs of red. One night I saw a multitude of black snakes piled up along a riverbank. I gasped and directly after saw red.

Well that is simply showing the energy intense up a channel with the sushumna also flowing...so keep going...the red could be a moment of survival that kicks in...or also could be simply an intense release of a burst of energy...in either case simply see it as you know don't feed it and let it go...you are simply watching the movie of the progression through the layers...

After an insight that brings me to the realization that I'm not this body, the body feels shocked, then there is darkness and stillness.

Good...

One night there was a bright green light in my head and I had trouble falling to sleep, it was so bright.

Once again simply become aware of the breath and let the attention rest there for a moment...the green is showing a resting within the heart area...that is good...just let the attention drop for a moment...

I'm continuing to question and keep my balance with each new experience. I continue to ask "What is this I?" I ask, "What is it like to be psychologically alone?" "Perceiving ourselves to be separate is the cause of suffering. What does this mean?" I tell myself I won't accept anything divisive. Still the thoughts come back, Ganga and it all begins again. With all these experiences and shocks it all starts up again. Yes, surrender and start again and again.

Yes...you simply continue to look at what is the I?...what is it composed of?...is it transient or constant? Only the Constant is the Source - anything other than that belongs to the empty phenomena of the transient realm called Maya...so good to hear from you...

As Ego Dissolves 3

Dear Ganga:
Namaste Dear One -

The other night I had this odd dream. I was back in the psych ward (Yikes!) and assigned to watch this really insane, dangerous patient. I was upstairs in the hospital by myself and the crazy man was in this rinky dink cage. It felt as if he could get out at anytime, so of course I didn't feel very safe up there all by myself. Then, he broke out of the cage and began to rush at me. I called downstairs for help and this very competent nurse I worked with in the psych ward (Corrie) and some others came up just in time. They all crowded around the crazy man and forced him back in his cage. The elevators stood open and Corrie told me to run, just to get out and she would handle it. I didn't waste any time leaving. I went down the elevators and out the door. Then I found myself running down all these cement staircases outside. There were trees all lined up on either side of the stairs and it was a warm evening. I remember I was wearing a lab coat. There were many other people running on these, what seemed like endless staircases. Some people were wearing scrubs and hospital attire. There was a sense of danger in the air, but nothing tangibly dangerous. We all just kept running for our lives, not looking back. Then at one point I was lifted straight up in the air. The breeze was calm and gentle and there was a great sense of peace. I was shocked to go from running, running, running with the others to this place of great stillness. It took me a second to realize that I could just lay back and relax and this is exactly what I did and the breeze carried me. I heard these words very loud in my head, "It's over. It's all over."

Yes...Yes...and once over it IS over...and That is it the Great sense of abiding Peace...sometimes you just have to be willing to let go of the world and its *problems* and dangers etc...and everyone Is running for their lives in some sense...once you can surrender it all totally you will in essence be pulled out...

Then I woke up and of course saw colors. My mind was quiet for time. Then the alarm went off very loud and I jumped up out of bed to start my day.

It is great that there was the still mind for a time...once it is seen the mind will still if not chased...it will remain in that stilled awareness...

I really want to thank you for your support. Working with you is my last stop. You provide all the direction and guidance an individual needs on this path and the rest is up to the individual. Sharing these experiences with someone that understands has decreased my fear immensely. Thank you.

Well it only works if one is willing to do the work and let go of the incidentals and not run away from them...am glad that you keep moving forward...you are doing very well and Will complete - of that I have NO Doubt....

As Ego Dissolves 4

Hello Dear Ganga:
Namaste Dear One -

Ganga, Is the witness different than the thing that one is observing? Who is the witness? Is it not the same as the thing (image, thought, whatever) that one is observing?

How could that be...? if you can see something how can it be what is being seen? What is it that is seeing? if you see the body then are you the body? is the body what is watching itself?

Indeed go into this WHAT is it that Witnesses? it does no good for me to answer this...it is of value when you can see the answer yourself...

Is it composed of the same thing? I understand intellectually and through insight that when the thing being observed is not there, the witness is also not there because there is nothing to witness. Mostly in the witness state there is a gap between the two. The witness and the thing being witnessed. Is this what 'self-consciousness' is?

Go into it...find out the answer...it will come...just observe it...

I am always conscious of my experiences, can recite it back to someone etc. If there is no self-consciousness, is memory gone?

What would remain to remember? When there is only ONE...

Is there anything to experience because the experiencer doesn't exist? Please explain.

Hahahahahaha...that is what you surrender to... To Find OUT the Answer to this question once and for All...

Today is a beautiful spring like day here. I sat on a park bench under a weeping willow tree for a long while. I'm getting a sense of a different reality flashing in here and there. My mind blanks out when I'm relaxed (almost trance like) and I'm only aware of the body laying on the bench, the various sensations, but I'm still conscious of this. Is this self-consciousness the same thing as what I'm observing? I welcome all of these experiences and am not afraid of them. I continue to do my work and mothering as if none of these odd experiences ever occurred or will occur again. I don't care really.

Good...simply see that there is witness...the I AM...what is beyond the witness? What makes the witnessing possible...?

Ganga, What is the 'I am'? Is it different than the 'I'? Aren't they the same? I think you talked about being aware of the 'I am' after the tunnel experience. Could you explain more about the 'I am'. Being aware one exists, Is this the 'I am'?

The I AM is the feeling of existence...but there is Source that is even stripped of the I AM...it IS but there is no 'I' cognition present...this is why you must continue on forward and continue to surrender to Source...

As Ego Dissolves 5

Hello Dear Ganga
Namaste Dear One -

I'm continuing to notice myself changing. What I notice is that it is very real that the 'I' is not real. It hits me quite strong sometimes, I notice the emptiness of thoughts and images, how they are continuous and break up immediately like clouds or blow away like dust when I come back to the I AM. I am shocked that I took all of this to be the world and related it to reality. It hits hard that I am evaporating, that it is real that the person is not real and is fading. There is fear sometimes, but the fear dissipates quickly when questioned.

Also, when I am quiet, there is the feeling that the world is fading, like it is moving away from me, yet there cannot be an 'I' that it is moving away from. All is more black, more dark. I question my senses all the time, my conclusions and perceptions. When tested much of the time they are wrong and if they appear right, what use is the extraneous information they bring? My attention may be focused on the way someone looks, what someone said or is talking about, the sound or color of and object and my mind wants to play on this all the time, to relate it immediately to the self. Spontaneously, however, it is all funneled towards eternity, moved in that direction like a one-way road or absorbed in quiet.

I view the body as a piece of nature, magnificent in its own way, yet subject to the laws of nature. Acceptance of nature feels well and right. To allow it to take its natural course, this too feels well and right.

The great witness is coming forward more. The body seems to be simply cradled by and in this witness, yet the witness has no feeling whatsoever for it. Still there is love. I am fading into this, letting down, letting go in it. It's stunning to me that the truth was here the whole time, that the simple power of awareness is all that is needed. The simplicity is astonishing.

One feels like a dog that's been chasing his tail for God knows how long and all the sudden he just stops the whole thing and sits quietly. One realizes instantly, the futility of the chase, and is only aware of the simplicity of being, that it is all perfect and well and always has been.

Kundalini energy easily twists, distorts images and puts them on a fast track in one's mind along with the sound effects, color and bright lights all at once. Also there is the pressure on various parts of the body, change in body perception and feeling like the floor is shaking. The explosions enter in here and there too and religious images.

It's difficult to stay with one's Beingness when this is happening. I can't find myself anywhere sometimes Ganga, but then I ask, "Who is looking?" I just want to return home. For this whole thing to come back on itself and be made right.

As Ego Dissolves 6

Hello Dear Ganga
Hello and Namaste Dear One -

When I went to lay down the other night, there was great pressure on my body from the energy surging through it. There was pressure on my chest, great pressure on my head and ears accompanied by a very loud ringing. My body felt heavy from the weight of it and my head turned to the side on its own. My bed was waving and it felt as if the whole house was tipping. I totally lost track of who I was. I had absolutely no idea who I was, I couldn't put anything in context, no past (thank God), no future.

The energy rushed up through me. My heart began to pound. Eventually, it all settled back down into the body again. I was unaware for a time of where I was or if I was anybody at all. Thoughts popped in here and there, but there was no context for it, like the fallout after an explosion. I wonder why I need to have so many of these experiences. Each one appears to further excavate the self, wash the consciousness clean until none of me remains. I remain passive, like a wide-eyed child because I don't know. I'm still functioning, but feeling very empty and carved out. The world appears so vivid and sounds are so loud. I know my experiences are very trivial compared the final communion.

It is the desire of my life to die and commune with that which is real.

It sounds like you are traveling the road of experience like that traveled by Bernadette Roberts[7]...it is coming...with each of these cleansings it is getting closer...just keep surrendering it is very very close...you are doing so well...just stay relaxed and open to seeing... don't look for a self just let it melt away... it feels strange at first but it becomes the norm in time...and you will be able to function no-one notices much externally...but your paradigm will simply go through a radical overhaul and a whole new paradigm will come into being...

*Take good care of yourself, as usual. All is fine here. I'm going to go into the quiet today. All is becoming clearer. Your words and presence always have been and are just right. Just perfect. I told K****, "All that Ganga tells you is totally and completely sufficient to complete this process. There's no need to look any further. Even one or two small statements she makes is enough. Take it and be quiet with it. That she has completed is enough".*

This is the key...to go into the silence and let it take root and in time fruition will come...but it doesn't come by intellectualizing it or attempting to pull it apart...it comes when one is willing to enter into the silence and to surrender...one surrenders either all at once or bit by bit it is pulled away...in either case it comes to the same final REALITY and Being...and when that emerges Liberation IS...

As Ego Dissolves 7 [Excerpt from letter]

Dear Ganga
Namaste Dear One -

---

[7] *The Experience of No-Self*, Bernadette Roberts, State Univ. of New York. 1993

Yes, the self is melting away here and there. I'm doing my best to stay out of the whole thing. I can't go beyond the I AM. It can't go beyond itself. There is something else that needs to take over now and this is not up to me. It does feel very strange not knowing who one is, but I can still write and respond and do things. You're absolutely right. No-one notices externally. No worries about looking strange to others.

Progressing towards our natural self should be what's normal. It's all so very challenging. I can only imagine a day without having to do this work.

One day it will come...a time of total surrender and then that will be it...the whole new paradigm will emerge...you are Very close...and doing Very Well...so all that may be said at this point is just to continue and to have the Faith that All things work together for good...that what gets stripped away is simply the baggage and what remains is a New Being that is Whole and Complete...what will remain is the Peace minus the revolving 'I' and the mind will be stilled ...When you have done all you can the Grace will take over and pull you in, stripping away the conditionings and bondages created by minds' identifications...Everything will become Clear and Apparent...I pray for that day to come for you soon...

As Ego Dissolves 8

Dear Ganga:
Namaste Dear One -

The self is progressively dissolving and then coming back to itself with its repetitive thinking, reflection and nonsense.

This is fine, just keep going and one day the self will not return...for you this falling away is coming closer with each moment...I can see it dissolving...soon the limitational self and mind will simply cease to return...and what will remain is what IS...

The no-self is quite different from witnessing the body with no thoughts or images. Thoughts appear like clouds, but this emptiness has no relation to them.

Yes...this is the stilled mind...this is what will remain...all phenomena is empty in nature and therefore Non-Dual...this is WHY Liberation has Nothing to do with being in form or out of form as form is simply Empty in Nature and always only the reflecting power of Source...

The things I thought mattered do not matter at all.

This is also true...the things the world chases no longer have any impact...they simply dissolve...life goes on and Life itself is the Great Mystery and is simply Pure Experience without attachments...it is Free and Full as it IS... no matter what outer show is being presented...

My dear Ganga this thing is really moving along to the great joy of my heart. When my son is near or I'm relating to another, I have no problem managing this.

hahahahaha...No you do not...words flow...the relative mind is not searching for answers or catagories or judgements...and yet what is needed is there...it simply comes from the silence and void into Being...that is all...there is no thought attached to it as others think of mind and thought... it is effortless...

When the no-self sustains itself...when this state sustains itself...is this completion?

hahahahahaha when you are There you will Know...When there are no longer questions...When there is only THIS...When the answers fall away and simply IS remains - without question or movement...When the power ends and simply the unadulterated Light of consciousness IS...Then That is the end of the Path...the end of the Search and the start of Life...

Thank you so much Ganga. The greatest gift to give you and the world is to complete.

As Ego Dissolves 9

Dearest Ganga:
Namaste Dear One -

So strange to be working with death and dying now during this last stage of my process. It is difficult to start a new job now. I sit in the meetings or drive around with the nurses as the self comes and goes. I don't know who is behaving, who is acting. When I am reading, the body and mind want to still and just sit and stare.

Yes, one comes to the point of where the attention is so within that there is seeing without seeing and hearing without hearing...there is movement but what is moving and what is acting? and yet it all gets done as it needs be...

During these times I do not feel like I am involved in this world at all and am surprised to have a body that I have to maneuver in and out of places. To try to have my mind memorize anything at this point does not work. All the new information being thrown at me at my job hopefully will come when it is needed.

What is needed will be there...there is no need to stress about anything at this point...simply continue on surrendering...the form does what it must...there is no need to actively attempt to guide or direct it... it moves according to its nature...

I am not like the other nurses so full of nursey knowledge and so very chit-chatty. It is very difficult for me to even talk sometimes, but this may just be part of my personality and not part of this process.

When one no longer chases the world and its objects what is there to speak of? Chit-chat falls away...it is part of the process...

I'm just going to go to my job daily and do the best I can without worrying about how I'm coming off. I've always delivered safe care to the patients and have made it this far. It is so very difficult. I can't even retain work as a priority in my mind.

So why is that difficult? Don't attempt to maintain it simply continue to move according to your nature...there is no need to control anything as you are finding out...what needs to unfold does and quite well... it is a fallacy that there needs to be an ego self that controls our actions and lives...the vasanas and samskaras can go on quite well without any intervention...what was set in motion will continue unimpeded...

About four nights ago, I woke up early in the morning and the consciousness was totally black and void. The lights and colors that I have been so accustomed to this past year were gone. I'm not sure if I'm explaining this very well because I'm not very good at all of the words involved in this process. I will explain this to the best of my ability because today I am only relying on memory. This black void remained in my consciousness so dark and expansive. I was only the observer of this experience, but there was no self-consciousness about it. My body remained as still as if it was dead and this void remained for what seemed like a very long time. I recall some fear, but I remained totally, effortlessly passive.

Good, you are traversing the last space before Realization...it is so very close...continue on until no self remains to fear...this is not the place yet of Source but it is close...you were observing a state of consciousness that is basically being blanked of former things...keep going until only Source remains...

After quite some time something changed and I came back to myself in a way I've never experienced before. The simplicity is beyond description. I felt as if a light was turned on, but there were no visual lights. All was so incredibly simple that I had to giggle. I couldn't believe it. There was a sense of completion unknown to me prior to this.

Yes...this is a glimpse of the Reality of Realization...of the living of it...the simplicity...when merged then the lights are gone...there is Light but it is not the light of seeing brightness but indeed the light of Primal Intellect without

152

Knowing...YES...this is a Glimmer of what the Reality of Self-Realization IS...

Now you KNOW that it IS...and IS possible...so let the rest go...

After a time thoughts came back and the headache of the work began again. This saddens me, but this is my process. My path. When thoughts come up such as: "I am very tired. I want this or that or I can't do this or that", a spontaneous response arises, "Who says this? Who is speaking? Who is talking now?" and it shifts immediately.

YES! Great spontaneous Self-Enquiry...YES...there is nothing to be saddened about...soon it will drop and not return...simply continue on...your Living Sadhana is bearing fruit...so very very close...

It is understood immediately that this is the I that is speaking and we are not going in that direction. This is unknown I tell myself. This is not up to me. When a thought comes such as: "what if I get depressed?" or "How much further do I have to go?" - there is no-one to get depressed, there is no-one to go back to, there is no-one to go any further and yet I'm not Realized.

No and you won't be...for Realization occurs when there is no one that remains to be Realized...hahahahahaha what remains is simply Source...Source is ever Realized and Cognized by itself alone...and itself has no self as such...You are very close to being pulled in and stripped bare of all the attachments called 'self-identity'...what remains is the Clear Light of Being...it is NOT a personage...although for practical purposes we use the term 'I' when speaking but there is no "I" that remains...there is no "I" that gets Enlightened...Enlightenment is being totally Blown out...wherein Only Source remains as it IS...then there are stages that happen when settling into Realization...

A few months ago I had several dreams about islands burning up. I would be in a very small boat rowing frantically to the island. There were huge waves splashing over me and I was sure I would die, but I didn't. Of course this island is the I AM, it is burning and there's nothing to go back to.

There is also nothing to die...very good dream... the islands of self are burning up until only Ocean remains... hahahahahahaha...Excellent...

All one can do is continue on and without question I will. It's all so very strange and yet there is no other way out of it. I want with my heart and soul to return to what is true. The I AM is not honest and true.

Then put the whole heart and soul to rest let them simply disintegrate into Source...Nothing is lost in the end... simply the idea of identity with form...All form is simply empty in nature...All Phenomena is simply the reflective playing out of the Potentialities of Source and it is endless within the transient and yet simply ONE Absolute beyond the playing out of form...The ego self is never God and yet God is ALL of Creation in Play...beyond God is Source...beyond I AM is the Infinite...

As Ego Dissolves 10

Namaste Ganga
Namaste Dear One –

I don't even know where I'm at anymore in the process Ganga. Some days I don't recognize when I'm not thinking. I don't recognize when the self is not there. It's all so very empty and clear and the body is just there. It's just doing this or that without me there at all.

Yes good...

So very strange. I'm able to recognize when I'm thinking and the 'I' returns, but not always the other way.

Witness needs I AM which is what all phenomena springs from... without I AM is simply seeing... Original Mind needs no witness...

Sometimes the consciousness doesn't seem contained in the head, it fills the entire room. It's not contained in the body at all.

No it never was... it never has been...Consciousness is ONE...

Every night before sleep and when I wake in the middle of the night, my ears have a high pitched ring, the energy runs up through my head. I'll be thinking about this or that and it just wipes the whole thing out, thoughts, the self and all. I could be anybody laying there or nobody at all.

Good, it is progressing...the falling away of the illusory self identity...the Nad (sound) may come and go on occasion...the energy will end once drawn into the Nirvikalpa or Clear Light...Clear Light beyond Light which illuminates that which is known...

Ganga, what do you see when you close your eyes before sleep? I see darkness, movement, light and colors, sometimes very vivid scenery: mountains, oceans, blue sky and clouds. Lately, I have been seeing less colors outwardly and inwardly.

The colors and movements will end...there is no thought as to what is seen...usually there is nothing that proceeds across the mind therefore the screen is blank...when mind moves then phenomena is seen...

I watch all of this play as if watching a t.v. screen. For is it not myself? When one is complete there is no screen to observe and no observer. I can only recall this now. It was true that there was nothing to observe when completion was known for a moment. The light of understanding was all that was present. There was no screen to observe, no me to be in the background. Still now when the self is lost or when it intermittently falls away, there is still a screen of black, white, colors etc. It is apparent the final is beyond consciousness. It can reside in the body, but it is not the body. It is beyond the body, the self and consciousness. How could it be me?

hahahahaha the 'you' has been merely the conditionings that have been taken to be the self identity...you are so close... you

155

have had a brief sight of it... just let the rest fall away until that simplicity and Original Mind remains...stripped clean and bare of all that gives the illusion of separation...One has always been this Eternal Source that wears no name or face or identity...the first projection is I AM or that which is termed God...beyond that is Source the Primal Potentiality...it is the Pregnant Void which all of Life is a minimal reflection of...beyond the you is THAT...

One evening when I woke up at night it was known that the seeker is self-interested. I know this is obvious, because we start where we are at. We start from the self which is all we know. The seeker is selfish. The seeker is the I, and the I is selfish. It was known that the seeker/Guru relationship is a concept. The seeker is a concept. The Guru, before the I AM is realized, is a concept. I was face to face with this concept. I realized this concept must be shattered.

YES! I am nothing that you are not...the separation has never been for ONLY THAT EXITS which is ever beyond forms' identifications...Pure Life minus conditionings...

At night before sleep I say to myself, "I am not the seeker. I am the Sage, the limitless." To stabilize in that. I renounce the self to you. The limitless, the eternal. Take all of me. I am not afraid. Take over me. I am not this body. To die now to you, to the limitless. I am not seeking my own private, protected world. I am seeking the universal one. Take all that is needed. The I does not know. The limitless knowing, I AM".

The Source is the great Unknowing...when THAT Unknowing is entered the rest will be stripped clean and be reborn...

I suppose I'm doing all that is needed now for there is really nothing to do at all. I can't believe I ever thought there was. I can't believe I ever believed I was the body and yet this is still not always known as fact. The I is so terribly stupid and dull and always will be. I'm so stupid at least I know I'm stupid, which is about all the I can know.

Good, then you are just a hair breadth away from Awakening...just continue on...so very soon...may you let go of the last vestiges of clinging and surrender it all...and then will come the great cosmic laugh that there was nothing to surrender at all...

As Ego Dissolves 11

Namaste Ganga
Namaste Dear One

The desire of the soul to return to its source is overriding my little anxieties and worries and progress continues (Thank God). Last night before sleep, the consciousness was black space, there was nothing, but this. All appeared the same inside as outside. The crown of the head opened up and there was an explosion. The self was lost to this. The I was confounded. There were glimpses of simplicity again (not fully complete) and even a sense of peace here and there. Peace is something very new.

Yes, the Peace is stilled and silent...it simply IS and remains As Such...Simply one thread remains...Once completed the Peace will remain paramount...it does not waver...not in the midst of the transient storms is it moved...although to others' perceptions the self may be in emotional upheaval where in fact there is really none...

The no-self is just empty, nothing. There has been no peace or rest during this long process. There is only peace in being now. It is all so very deep and separate from what was thought to be known. It cannot be written down in words as you fully understand.

Yes, words cannot convey when there is no longer a within or a without...when all has fallen away and simply IS remains...when mind is stilled as chases no longer any illusion or play...when complete there is simply rest that remains...Peace...the transient play is merged and at One in the ever present stillness of Source... Not two...Not two...

To become one with the Guru, with Christ. To forget the Guru and become that.

Hahahahahaha…yes…where is the separation? No need any longer Guru and Self are not two…they have always been simply THAT…others take them to be something other as viewing form…but no form is cognized as they perceive it…it is for that One an empty phenomena…

There is no fear during this process thanks to your loving support. I was skiddish about the whole thing prior. Now the self doesn't matter to me at all. There is no investment in it, no gain. It provides nothing.

What a change from less than a year before… remember that fearful soul that sat trembling in abject fear… Where have they gone? what has been lost? there was nothing to lose but the illusions of fear and separation…

As Ego Dissolves (the Void and "I") Last Letter
Letter - the Void and "I"

Dearest Ganga
Namaste Dear One

In the many months since I last wrote to you, I have experienced much.

Yes indeed, it has been… but am glad to hear from you now…

I have been doing the 'Who am I?' enquiry.

Yes, good…

I have 'deconstructed' *I* till only awareness remained. Many times, I have experienced a Void where *I* didn't exist. Then coming back from this emptiness, an *I* would emerge, devoid of any identification. Afterwards, around the *I*, this present persona would assemble itself.

Why do you once again reconstruct it? perhaps it arises due to looking for it... there is nothing to look for but simply to Be..

The inverse also happens. Enquiry into Who am I? would bring me to experiencing *I* as simply energy, existing nowhere, in no time.

Ah yes, the First Dynamic...beyond that is the Void...

Sometimes as I go beyond my present personality, my brain creates other ME's, other personas. I experience myself as being of either gender, of any age, in any culture, in any time period. I 'see' surroundings, I 'feel' attachments, I 'am' this other person.

Interesting sidelines...these types of things may rise...but simply see the common thread that runs through it all...

Using my oh-so-limited meat-brain to understand this phenomena, I concluded that my mind needs to assemble human personalities, needs to exist in some human time and culture. I include the word 'human' because my mind didn't create non-human personas.

Any desire brings with it some semblance of form... there is nothing wrong in this but is simply the case...

Going beyond the various personas which my mind creates, I reach a state of simple awareness, where thought expressed in words is not possible. I then force myself to evaluate the experience.

Why? In this evaluation it brings separation into subject object again...

I conclude that there still is a very limited sense of *I* since my mind brings back the memory of the experience, though at those moments, I can't even recall my name, let alone other details of this present personality.

Good...don't seek the rest again...let them simply drift away...they aren't needed and all will be fine...

Then, coming out from this state of awareness, there comes a consciousness of *I* once more. Then sometimes, a fraction of a second questioning as to which personality *I* will become. And then this persona is reassembled from nothingness.

Yes, all comes from nothingness and lives within emptiness...but why to reconstruct anything...? simply accept what is as it is without covering...

Once I saw *I* as a silver thread emerging from the Nothingness, then this thread acted as a magnet, pulling towards itself a personality.

Hahahahaha...darn personality...not that there is anything wrong in it...others will always see some type of a personality but there is really nothing that you need to cling to or re-invent...

Quite a few times in the past month, I have erroneously believed myself to be Enlightened. Not because of the experiences, because nearly every day for the past year I have had experiences while meditating. It was because of how I felt for many days after certain experiences of Nothingness. Time was so fluid. There were periods of no-thoughts, of inner emptiness. There were no attachments. Things happened around me as if in a dream. My sense of *I* felt so weak as to disappear at times.

When it has quite gone Then...but you are very close...then life goes on as it is...neither clung to nor pushed away...but simply empty in nature like a dream...

Then after a few days, I would come back to a more 'normal' state and realize that I was not Enlightened after all. Hahahaha...

But you are close...I think what is happening is the fact that you are still making it a separate experience... and not letting it remain as is...

That's when my mind would try to convince me that all this 'Realization stuff' was bull, was nonsense, that I was wasting my time, that my life had no meaning and never would... and so forth.

The dramas of this personality were paraded before me. This always happens in the early morning, either just as I'm waking up, or the thoughts actually wake me up. Such are the mind's games and its arsenal.

So you need to cut the tree at the root of identity and then don't water it again...let it go...you are so close but then back away looking for another *identity*...once you can let go of it and not take it back it will remain as that *fluid* nature that you experienced...

I realize that my meat-brain cannot make sense of the Void in any way possible and yet it tries, just like all the other meat-brains try.

That is because the brain is Not within the void...it is filled with relative knowledge like a computer disc...you are not this physical brain at all...

When I am in simple awareness, beyond thoughts, it feels RIGHT, TRUE, TOTAL, PERFECT.

Then let it remain without looking for something else...

And because of these feelings, I now distrust all words, all thoughts, all mental constructions for they originate from human meat-brains.

They arise due to the clinging to past conditionings and events...let them go...but yes Truth is beyond all words, thoughts, and constructs... in This you are correct...

The only thing which I read which feels true is the description of Void. The only words so far that I've read that speak clearly of this experience, are yours and Sri Ramana Maharshi's.

and you will KNOW it as it IS...just relax into it and surrender 100% and accept...

Here are some thoughts which I wrote in an email I intended to send to you on January first, which I never did.

Ok…

There is nothing to know which is permanent except the Source of phenomenon, nothing to control for all slips like water through the fingers.

There is no reason to life, nothing to understand. There is no good nor evil, no dark nor light for these are constructions of human meat brains based on human experiences. The more one tries to understand, the less one will understand, the more chances of falling into more endless illusions.

Hahahahaha…good…yes…in trying to understand them you simply give them a valid nature…wonderful…

This is what is scary, the ultimate fear: that nothing can be known, nothing can be made sense of, nothing to hold on to, no supreme being to ask help from, no divine plan. All IS perfection, yet not the perfection that the human mind would want, not the sense that the human mind wants.

Yes, this is true…we want a benevolent father that sits and hands out sweets…but the Truth is that we are in control of our own destinies due to the karma of our own creation…it IS perfect…and it Can be changed by letting go of the illusions…the Nothing that is to be Known is Complete as IS…

There is nowhere to hide, nothing to believe, no rituals to do.

One must accept that one is simply human, a package of meat, that everything that one cherishes is illusion. There is no soul, no karma, no justice. We are totally powerless as human beings as long as we believe that all phenomena should and must have a meaning and logic and should have an inherent morality which our human minds can comprehend.

Oh, but we can and will move within a Satvik Harmony once the Truth is known...this is the path of mankind - to see and learn Love and Compassion - Gratitude and Bliss...Phenomena is what you make of it... it is either Divine or Demon...Heaven or Hell...it simply is the realm of transient experience...Soul is the belief and clinging to form and name...

We use a lot of energy trying to hold ourselves together, to hold our thoughts, our beliefs, our fears, our loves, our personas in place. When we let go of self, we experience a deep relaxation which we can experience as bliss, love and other powerfully positive feelings. The inverse is true also: when we cultivate deep relaxation, we let go of self.

YES...

We experience 'wellness' when we hold on to nothing, when we become IS-NESS, Being, simply energy floating without creating more swirls of energy with our thoughts.

Anything that is created by energy is ever in flux...it is moving and changing...beyond and permeating and surrounding that energy is Source...even the energy has an empty value to it...

There are many ways to become IS-Ness: through meditation, through self-inquiry, through body movements, through relaxation techniques, through sleep and what we ingest in our bodies, through practicing detachment from all, through concentrating on blissful, peaceful and loving feelings.

or letting it all go and surrendering to what IS...

The mind will experience moments which seem like insights, but one must be careful not to dwell on these, not to engage the mind in speculations on these insights. A waste of time for many of these insights will appear contradictory to the mind and engaging the mind is counter-productive.

Hahahahaha...YES...again very good...insights are of the relative...and all relative is change...

A moral person will find the road difficult because one will find that morality has no meaning outside of our human lives, outside of our culture and our place in time.

It is a societal conditioning...but the inverse is true then True LOVE may come and shine for one KNOWS that all is simply the Divine...

True compassion comes to the fore...

A person who prizes justice will find there is no justice.

Karma is total justice...that is the law of the universe and One...

A person who prizes love will find that love is only an experience that our mammalian bodies experience and has no meaning in itself.

It has simply the meaning that one ascribes to it...but when simply the Satvik remains it IS...no longer the love of the world but the Love of the celebration of Self with Self...it is a more generous love than that of the worldly persuasion...

A person who prizes logic will find that nothing is logical.

As it is being stripped away it appears so... but then perfect logic steps in...

A person who prizes knowledge will find that there is nothing to know.

Yes...all that is to be known is Source...the rest is icing on the cake...

A person who prizes order will find there is no order.

There is an order to the universe - this is why karma is undefeatable...

People looking to find esoteric knowledge will be disappointed or will simply lose themselves in mind games.

hahahahaha...esoteric knowledge is as vast as the mind...whatever one seeks may be created...but to what avail? In that sense yes, they really hold no meaning...

People looking to control what will happen in their lives, whether they will find riches or love will also be disappointed or lose themselves in mind games.

What need is there to control anything? All is transient within this realm...yet Eternal in the Grand scheme...so what to control...?

There is nothing to know, nothing to understand, nothing to be.

There is no path in life, no reason for being, no predetermined outcome, no spiritual meaning. There is no past nor future. Time is part of phenomena, creation and illusion.

The illusion is the conditioned limitation...Life is Grand as it is...

What matters if we die? If our culture dies? If our species or planet disappears? We are flecks of dust in the unknowingly immense dust bunny.

hahahaha...and if it ends another will arise as this is the nature of Source...

I see everything as swirls endlessly creating more swirls. Creation abhors repeating itself, so no two are ever exactly the same: galaxies, planets, people (even identical twins or clones), snowflakes, leaves, even molecules.

Yes, creation is Eternal...the vast Pregnant Void is endless in its nature...it gives the ability for creation to move as it will...and yet within that, everything is held to the patterns of karma and divine unfolding balance...

No two thoughts are ever the same.

Everything is born and dies in every moment...

All thoughts are created, all thoughts are swirls of energy.

Yes...

Everything is illusion.

The substance of dreams...neither real nor unreal...illusion is the minds taking it to be the very limited seen...what is seen is temporal...changing yet created and sustained from the Eternal Unchanging One...

The mind is endlessly fascinated with creation. It loves the game.

Yes, the form gets caught up in the play and loses the sight of Eternal One...

Counting all the manifestations of creation and cataloging them, trying to control and manipulate the creations. It likes to be the big fish in a little pond, the little king over its kingdom of baubles (what I know, what I've experienced, what I understand, what I value...).

A king within his domain...a mind within his universe...and in this he limits his world...to the known and seen...

The little king believes it can know God, it can understand the why of creation, the how. When trying to do this, the mind simply creates more illusions.

Yes...

Sri Ramana said there is no *I* when you fall asleep and that is one's true state. He said that being awake or dreaming is all the same thing.

Yes, both the substance of dreams and minds' creation...

I understand this now because in both states, there is the belief that there is an *I* experiencing something and an outside to be experienced. There is no *I*, no inside nor outside.

There are no two states but simply one continuous Being...there is no inner nor outer... no separate other...no coming and going...

I had mistakenly thought that Void was aware of *I* since *I* was aware of Void. But when I am in Void, there is no resonance of *I*; it is not a two-way street.

Right...Void has no awareness except IS...no relative knowledge...whole and complete...no time...no space...simply Source...

I had also mistakenly believed that Awareness was aware of awareness, was curious about awareness, was concerned about awareness. But in Awareness, there is no awareness of *I*. So I don't understand nor do I 'feel' why some people say that God is playing hide and seek with himself. There seems to be no awareness of Bigger to Smaller, if I may put it that way. Void is unaware and unconcerned with anything.

Hahahahaha…right...only manifestation is concerned with itself...but all manifestation is the infinite unfolding Source...not two...

Not Two...it is empty in nature and ever non-dual...Not Two...

A side-note, I don't experience the heart chakra or any chakra anymore. I had been pursuing 'Who am I?' into the heart chakra for a long time when one day, the *I* and the heart chakra disappeared and I was left with 'Self' and emptiness inside my body, and this emptiness remains with only a vague resonance where the heart chakra was.

Right...this will mellow and Love will be once you discover that creation and Source are Not Two...Not Two...this comes in time...first all is drawn back in, stripped clean and then spit out within the paradigm of Not Two and that it is perfection as it is the infinite Mystery of Being...

So now I find myself in a place where I believe totally there is nothing to Know or experience except Void, nothing to trust or believe except Void yet I don't have the emotional detachment which Enlightenment brings. I'm still 'me'. I go from caring what happens to 'me' to experiencing that there is no 'me' to care about. I go from being comforted by Nothingness to being bothered that there is Nothingness. I go from Knowing there is nothing to know, to still wanting to understand and make sense of something.

There is a further step to take...a richness that will come...a further unfolding to come...be patient...wait and see what emerges...

I thank you for being my Guru and am extremely grateful. I read all your posts in Kundalini Online, God Realized, Guru Satsang and you for being my Guru and am extremely grateful. I read all your have now joined the Meditation group to read you there. I resonate to your words and your approach to guiding others. For me, you are enlightenment personified.

Hahahaha...there are others that may agree and others that disagree but such is the world...I am so glad you are here...just have faith...relax, totally surrender and see what emerges...it gets infinitely richer... the Mystery is yet to emerge...

Afterword

Special Reminders

Namaste and thank you for allowing me to share this book with you...The first and foremost thing that I would like to address is this: please do not chase after a kundalini awakening as a way to solve your problems. It simply is not. It is not a way to collect siddhis and not something that can be controlled like turning on and off a light switch... If you already are in the midst of a kundalini awakening by all means find a reputable guru/guide that has had a kundalini awakening and has successfully 'completed' the journey and rests within Self-Realization. And yes, they are few and far between. There are many, many gurus but few whom have travelled and completed a kundalini path. If you feel a 'strong shakti' coming from a guru it does not mean that they are completed and in fact, it may be a good indication that they are still within the midst of the journey. You will feel a gentle and calming energy around a completed one, along with a sense of stillness and balance.

Don't go to someone that is teaching kundalini yoga and expect to find reliable help - most have simply theories. A kundalini yoga class and a competent guru/guide are two separate things. Don't go to a reiki healer that is in the midst of an awakening - their energy will be unstable at best. Use caution when doing anything that has to do with increasing the energy. Be careful with starting any type of intensive yogic asana classes as well. Easy stretching is fine. Don't do pranic breathing exercises unless you are under the guidance of a qualified guru.

Make sure that you do not tax your body. Get enough sleep and do constant relaxation measures. Understand that every situation that comes up is transient and will change.

Always follow the middle path and stay grounded and centered. It really is a must before starting to pull away at the ego identity.

I sincerely pray that all who enter into the path of kundalini have a successful and gentle journey. May those that successfully complete find it within their hearts to help others to completion. There are now more and more awakening in order to traverse the cellular memories and collective consciousness to awaken to a new paradigm and dimension. The completion, while the end of the search, is simply the start of life. What remains is the flow of the rivers of living waters which, once tasted, keeps one forever refreshed...The Peace Which Passes all Understanding is a Reality. The still and silent mind is a Reality.

If any know of competent individuals or gurus that are indeed taking others to balance and completion please contact me with their information so that an ongoing information line may be set up... I hope to one day have a facility where others may come to stay and learn to balance and be able to continue on in their lives in a meaningful way.[8]*

PATHWAY

May i walk the path in humility
May my mind be focused on my goal.
May i see and correct my own faults,
leaving my brothers and sisters to correct their own.
May my lips speak only wisdom.
May my hands give only kindness.
May my feet walk in peace.
May my eyes see purity wherever i look.
May my heart find joy in all that i do...
May my constant prayer be that all beings find a Path
  to God and enlightenment...

---

[8] *Since this writing, the ashram has been founded.

Addition to Previous Edition

September, 2005

Namaste –

As the first edition of this book was published three years ago, I can now share with you in this edition, some findings and what is taking place since...

I have found that when completed and resting within total balance that to give initiation and Shaktipat to those who are already activated can aid in bringing them into a better alignment and balance. First though one has to make sure that the potential Sadhakas are given a good foundational understanding and that the fears that can lead to paranoia and psychosis are assuaged. I hear of the casualties - those who have been given Shaktipat without this guidance...and then there are those who are on the edge of paranoia...a shift in energy can continue to send them over the edge...

I have found that continued hands-on energy sessions, given through Zero Point Siddha Energy Cellular Release and Balancing method, helps to move Sadhakas through kriyas and blocks to a balanced unfolding. (The 0 Point (SECRB) healing methodology is taught and open to those who are geared towards the whole of the Kundalini path. In order to work on kundalini-activated cases the healer has to first reach an inner stillness with the ability to be 'in sync' with the energies and without projecting or being sucked into others' dramas.)

I have found that a falling away is happening among the Sadhakas (as opposed to the implosion of surrendering all at once).

When entering into this Kundalini path, Diksha (initiation of Shaktipat) is given. Mantras are infused and activated. Ongoing guidance and instruction is given. One of the requirements is for ongoing contact for monitoring of the unfolding consciousness. Meditation is required as well as active living

Sadhana (spiritual practice within life) such as Karma Yoga, Bhakti Yoga, and Jnana Yoga (which is Knowledge gained from Direct Experience)... this is not a path engaged in for physical health (such as touted by Hatha) or as a hobby... it is a full on path that is geared for those who are committed to a Life that uses each moment and breath as an opportunity for spiritual growth, to go beyond the conditioned persona and suffering...I offer guidance to those who are willing to dive in fully.

It is my heart's joy to see a vanguard of spiritual adepts coming to the forefront as humanity is evolving. More workers need to be in place to aid others to reaching the fullness of their journeys. It is time to extend the modalities that bring balance rather than continuing to watch the fracturing and instability that takes place when the blind attempt to lead the blind...

Love - Light - Great Peace - Abundant Life & IS
Swami Ganga-Puri Kaliuttamananda-Giri

From the Initiates...
Diksha and 0 Point Energy Work

Diksha experience (Avlokita, July 2005)

...I had a hundred questions to ask Swami-G about what I was going to be going through during and after initiation. However, in her presence, my mind stilled. My sense of time vanished.

I did let Swami-G know how terrified I was about shaktipat. My kundalini experiences thus far had been very subtle as they were just stirrings - I was afraid that shaktipat would cause an overload of energy. Swami-G started me off by just meditating with me. I had never seriously meditated before, but the experience was nothing short of AWESOME. I remember closing my eyes saying to myself, *this isn't going to work.* Then my mind stilled and I was taken somewhere deep. I don't know where, I can't remember what was seen....but after I was brought out of meditation I didn't know where I was, what day it was or where I had gone. After my head quit spinning, I asked if it was always that intense. Swami-G told me that normally, being in the presence of a guru deepens the experience. After that, there was no question in my mind as to whether I should take diksha or not. About an hour later, the ceremony began.

During diksha, tears flowed the whole time. I sat down and Swami-G poured beautiful mantras over me. My first reaction when I felt the energy rise, was absolute fear. Fear from all the warnings I had read about dealing with the kundalini. I wanted to run. But I continued sitting and surrendered myself to God. Then love washed over me as she continued touching different chakra centers. By the end of it I was laughing and more alive then I had ever felt. Light flames of heat were wrapped around the sushumna and there was nothing else in the world I could ask for more than that.

On Diksha and balance (Jaba, summer 2005)

Diksha has brought balance with a capital 'B'. It has removed the fear of Kundalini manifestations. When there is a big release or discharge, the diksha mantras bring everything back into balance, peace and being aware in the moment. I no longer feel like I'm stuck in the movie *Groundhog Day* - repeating the same experiences over and over and never really being able to move on. And no matter what happens, Swami-G is there to guide and support.

The more I use and listen to the diksha mantras, the sweeter they become...like every level of my being is being washed in Love and nourished at the deepest levels. Diksha is priceless...there is no real life until that grace is received...a living grace, not a momentary bliss.

On Energy Work (Poorna, August 2005)
Coming to the ashram has been a big 'letting go'. To finally accept that I can let go of pain. Even more than that - to finally accept that I do not need to put myself *through* pain in order to be free of it. Here is a way to just let it go.

The 'tune-up' is given while I am sitting. Swami-G moves her hands over the chakras from both the front and back of my body. Here is someone with whom this goes beyond trust. I feel myself sigh within and let go. Often, big blocks are broken through - sometimes with a sudden jolt. It is all so very quick and powerful and the effect is always the same - whatever had been disturbing the peace before just quite simply is not there anymore. I feel peaceful and grounded.

The energy work is given by Swami-G and Siddhananda whist I am laying down. 'Divine' is an apt word for this experience. Taking a dream ride on a magic carpet. The intensity does increase when Swami-G places her hands in proximity of my head - as if there is a contraction, everything is drawing up. At the same time, Siddhananda may be at the feet where a release of energy is felt running down the legs and dispersing at the feet. Finally, Swami-G brings everything back to the heart again. The result after this is that I feel 'lighter'. Freer.

Before coming to the ashram and taking diksha, my past practice was Vispassana meditation. With this method I found I was able to bring pain/blocks into awareness and watch the energy dissipate. However to reach the awareness necessary to dissolve the pain would require four of five days of sitting, cross-legged on the floor for up to fourteen hours a day. Even then, this could only take things so far as the deeper the blocks went, the deeper into stillness I needed to go in order to once again continue the clearing process. With the energy work, all that is needed is to lie down and relax! Swami-G works from 0 point balance. It seems that by surrendering to that stillness in which she is settled, that which would literally take months (maybe years!) to clear through intensive Vispassana meditation, is dissolved in that one session.

On Diksha

After a week at the ashram, there wasn't even any question about whether to take diksha or not - this coming from someone who *never* thought they would end up with a guru!

During the ceremony there was simply peace. For a couple of days afterwards, I was aware of the kundalini spiraling in what felt like clear space. Layers and layers effortlessly dissolving. Repeating the mantras would sometimes initiate that drawing up of the energy as experienced during the energy work. Also when looking at a photograph of Swami-G, there is a stirring at the heart chakra.

December 2005

...Often now all is just crystal clear 'space'. Sometimes ripples are 'seen' and if thoughts are then followed, there is darkness and a sense of 'I' returns...sometimes the force of energy releasing draws the mind in this way. Other times, when walking along, even the emptiness warms into an Isness...a delicious Oneness...

A Call To The Medical Community

It is time for the medical community to begin to update its outlook from simply checking off a list of symptoms to looking at the whole picture. While going through the kundalini experience, being labeled with various mental diagnoses did not help the process at all - in fact it made it much more difficult to see through the rising upheavals as transitory. It is frightening to think you may be losing your sanity and then have a label attached and toxic medications given. Not only are you in fear, but then with a foggy mind, even more toxic dramas emerge.

One has a tendency to buy into labels and that is a large part of the problem. Everything is categorized and labeled to fit into a nice neat package, but within the kundalini process there is no easy ribbon to place on it. What distinguishes kundalini from temporal lobe epilepsy or from the various mental health professional labels is that this process is one that can and will, with proper care and understanding, take one to total well being. It does not end in a psychotic break from reality unless misunderstood and labeled with the patient then drugged into a psychotic state of confusion.

So what is needed at this juncture is: to run an EEG to make sure there is not temporal lobe epilepsy; to perhaps have an MRI run to make sure there is not a tumor or an organic cause; to do an evaluation for schizopherina. Then look at the whole picture. Does this patient have a multitude of the symptoms of kundalini awakening?[9] If so, then they need to be assured that they are not crazy or suffering from some great abnormal condition. The best thing to do is to give them support and send them to a professional who knows what kundalini is and what its ongoing process entails.

In kundalini crises what is needed is: to have a heavier dietary regime; to be able to see that the rising phenomena is transitory; to be able to learn to enter into a relaxed state; to be able to step back and disassociate from the rising phenomena, and to come back into a grounded and fully aware body state.

Clearly, there is an ever expanding need for psychologists who are trained in kundalini intervention care. This takes specialized understanding of the process along with a method to

---

[9] See Chapter: Kundalini – Signs and Symptoms

navigate the clients into a place of self-care with support. This process is not the same as confronting old issues and bringing them to closure. This process needs to be approached from a whole new dynamic - one of breaking free from the identification with conditionings. (May I urge you to read 'Ego Bondage and Illusions of Truth' which addresses *how* conditionings are formed and what is needed to break through.)

There are more and more people having kundalini awakenings every day and therefore an increasing need for competent care.[10]

Thank you for your care and attention in expanding your knowledge in this field.

---

[10] In a 2005 survey carried out online among forum readers, 68% of those with active kundalini now know someone with whom they have regular contact, who has since had kundalini become active.

GLOSSARY

Advaita: Not two, Non-Dual. The Philosophical viewpoint that the Ultimate Reality is but a single Essence or God from which all life and manifest existence arises, abides in, and returns to, and cannot be separated from. A monistic theosophy.

Agape Love: Christian term for generalized (non-personal) love.

Ajna chakra: Third eye

Alpha – Omega: Beginning – End.

Ananda: Bliss - The joy of God-consciousness.

Asana (Assana): Seat. In Hatha yoga refers to the many yogic postures designed to stimulate and balance the subtle energies of mind and body.

Ashram: A holy sanctuary. The place of residence and or teaching center of a Saint, Satguru or Sadhu.

Astral realm: Subtle realm. Non-physical plane of existence.

Atman: The Soul in its entirety, the individual life essence. Also sometimes used to refer to the universal Self or Spirit.

Bhagavan: Godly, Divine, Sacred Glorious. Used in relation to Gods and Divine Beings such as Krishna, Gautama Buddha and Sri Ramana Maharshi.

Bhakti: Devotional worship, faith, love and surrender to God, an aspect of God or Guru.

Bhakti Yoga: The path of devotion and surrendering until the ego is totally effaced. Union with love.

Brahmachari: One who is devoted to the life of a religious student requiring self-discipline, fidelity and abstinence etc.

Chakra: Wheel. Energy centers within the human subtle energy network where energy channels and meridians converge. The seven major chakras run along the spine from base to cranial chamber and correspond approximately with the major nerve ganglia in the physical body.

Brahman: Absolute.

Brahmin: Priestly class (Hindu).

Chela: The spiritual disciple of a Guru.

Chitta: Memory; mind.

Chod: Ceremony performed by Buddhists to prove illusion of form by confronting fears.

Conscious Awareness: Being in the moment with here and now.

Darshan: Vision. A mystical exchange of energy through the eyes between Holy entity, such as Temple Deity or Guru and spiritual seeker. Much sought after within Hindu culture.

Dark Night of the Soul: Tribulation/suffering phase of growth.

Diksha: Spiritual initiation into a lineage or practice usually by transmission of Shakti from Preceptor to student resulting in an initial or deeper connection between the two.

Duality: *See* Dvaita

Durga: Archetype. The one who fights negativity – 'demonic' aspects of mind.

Dvaita: The theosophy of dualism or pluralism in which God and the soul are seen as eternally separate. The opposite of Advaita. Attachment to transient world.

Five names: Of the Sikh tradition.

Formless Constant: Descriptive term for Absolute.

Ganesh: The Lord of Categories and obstacles. The elephant-faced Mahadeva worshipped for his great wisdom and invoked before beginning any venture. One who breaks through obstacles.

Grace: Not by effort. Grace IS when the 'doer' is out of the way.

Gunas: Qualities. The three fundamental qualities that make up the nature of manifest existence. They are; **Satvic** - reflecting the light of pure consciousness, rarified and translucent; **Rajas** - inherent in energy, movement, action and passion; **Tamas** - inertia, density and darkness, the force of contraction and dissolution.

Guru: Weighty One. A term that can be used to denote an authority on any given subject, most commonly refers to one of spiritual knowledge, Refers to both the outer form of Guru and the inner and ultimately supreme Guru. A SatGuru is a spiritual preceptor.

Hari Om Tat Sat: Praise be That eternal Truth.

Hatha Yoga: Yogic practice involving physical postures and breathing exercises designed to stimulate and balance the mind and subtle energy systems of the body.

Japa: Incantation. The repetition of mantra or names of deities, intoned either silently or aloud.

Jivanmukti: Liberation while one is alive.

Jnana: Wisdom or knowledge. The wisdom gained when the soul reaches full maturity, it is not an intellectual knowledge gathered through study, but a direct knowing attained through realization of Parasiva.

Jnana Yoga: Union with wisdom.

Kali: The fierce aspect of Shakti represented by a black and naked Goddess garlanded with skulls. She is the champion of sadhana and the Mother of Liberation.

Karma: Action or Act. The Universal law of action and reaction or cause and effect, and the fruits of those actions or subsequent effect returning to the one carrying out the deed. As you sow so shall you reap.

Karma Yoga: The path of selfless service. Union with service.

Krishna: Personalized form of God or Avatar.

Kriya: Action. An involuntary physical movement of the body or limbs caused by arousal of the Kundalini.

Kundalini: The primordial cosmic energy lying dormant within every individual at the base of the spine, analogous to a coiled serpent. When aroused she enters the sushumna in the center of the spine, ascending to pierce each chakra or level of consciousness as she climbs to the crown chakra where shakti unites with Shiva.

Lila: The play of God.

Lingam: *See* Shivalingam.

Lucid dreams: Consciously aware of dreaming while dreaming – therefore able to interact.

Mantra: A syllable word or phrase that has been infused with special power by the preceptor, usually at initiation. Used for Japa can be chanted silently or aloud as an aid to stilling the mind and to invoke deities and certain siddhis.

Mara: *See* Maya

Mass mind memory: Thoughts and awareness held in place by mankind in general.

Maya: Relative reality. The realm of manifestation and creation, and that which deludes the soul into believing the manifest to be the ultimate reality. Sometimes interpreted as 'illusion', veiling the soul's true nature.

Mudras: Seal. Specific hand movements or gestures usually expressing power, of both symbolic and practical use. An essential part of dance, certain yoga practices and religious ritual.

Nad: Internal sound.

Nadi: Subtle energy channels within the inner body connecting the many chakras, there are reputedly 72,000 nadis. The three major nadis are; **Ida** - running parallel to and on the left of the spine - it is pink, downward-flowing and the feminine or moon aspect; **Pingala** - parallel and on the right of the spine - it is blue, upward flowing and the sun or male aspect; **Sushumna** - running up the center of the spinal cord and is the conduit for the passage of Kundalini.

Neti-Neti: Not this, not that. A process of negating thoughts and events that arise in the mind until all that remains is Source.

Nirvikalpa (Sahaja, Keevala) Samadhi: *See* Samadhi

No-self state: No holding in the consiousness of an individualized persona.

Non-Duality: Monistic Theism - *see also* Advaita

Om /Aum: The first emanation and sound of Creation. The primordial sound pervading all manifest existence. The most Sacred of Hindu mantras, said by some to be the first name of God. It can also be used to infer "yes" or "verily", and is often use to precede or as an ending to other words in a mantra.

Om Namah Shivaya: "Praise Lord Shiva". The Panchakshara mantra, at the center of the Yagur Veda, the second of the original three Vedas it can be said to be at the very Heart of Hinduism and is Supreme among Shaivites. The five syllable mantra; Na is the Lord's veiling grace; Ma is the world; Shi is the world; Va is His revealing Grace and Ya is the soul.

Prana: Vital energy or life principle from the root pran (*to breathe*). There are five vital airs or pranas within the human body which form all other bodily energies. Prana is also sometimes used to denote the cosmic or universal life force.

Pranayama: The movement and manipulation of bodily energies through breathing exercises and breath control.

Pranic surges: quick surge of energy that recedes.

Puja: A rite of worship performed in the Temple or home, performed towards consecrated objects, its intention being to purify the atmosphere and create a connection to the inner worlds, thus invoking the presence of God, Deities or Sat Guru.

Rajas: *See* Gunas

Reiki: A spiritual practice established in early 20th century Japan by Mikao Usui, based predominately on the transmission of energy, and since hijacked within Western culture to become almost exclusively an energy healing practice.

Radha: Devoted to Krishna.

Sadhaka: A serious spiritual aspirant who performs sadhana and is usually under the guidance of a Guru.

Sadhana: Spiritual discipline or practice such as meditation, yoga, japa, puja, austerity etc, to facilitate purification of the mind and subsequent spiritual unfolding.

Sadhu: Perfect, complete. A good and virtuous holy man - a saint.

Sage: A Self-Realized or Liberated Being.

Saivite (Shaivite): One who follows the religion of Saivism and worships Lord Siva (Shiva) as the Supreme. It is the oldest of the four sects of Hinduism and records can be traced back at least 8000 years to the Indus valley.

Samadhi: A contemplative or meditative state of consciousness in which the one who meditates and the object of meditation are united as one. The highest state of samadhi is **Nirvikalpa** samadhi where there is no awareness of form or senses and that which is beyond time, space and form (Parasiva), the Eternal One resulting in a total transformation of the individual consciousness. **Sahaja** Samadi is that which comes naturally and is present always.

Samskaras: The latent impressions from past experiences in this or a previous birth which vibrate in the strata of the subconscious coloring our thoughts and actions.

Sanskrit: Ancient language.

Sanyasi: An ascetic who has renounced the world and all worldly affairs in order to facilitate vigorous and dedicated pursuit of the spiritual path and Self Realization to the exclusion of all else. A Hindu Swami or monk who has taken Sannyasa Diksha initiation.

Satchitananda/Sat Chit Anand: Existence or Truth/Consciousness/Bliss. The state of being of Parashakti or the mind of the ever transcendent Lord Shiva, and the simultaneous state of existence of the individual soul body.

SatGuru: (*see* Guru) A spiritual preceptor who has achieved spiritual perfection and union with Parashiva through Nirvikalpa Samadhi.

Satsang: Association with Truth. Being in the presence of a Satguru or Realized Being for the purpose of spiritual knowledge and study.

Satvic: *See* Gunas

Self: The Absolute, Parasiva, God. That which gives life to all existence, the One without a second.

Self-Enquiry: Process of transcending illusion of persona as separate from Self. i.e. absolute

Self-Realization: Union with the Self through Nirvikalpa Samadhi

Seva: *See* Karma Yoga

Shaivite: *See* Saivite

Shakti: Energy or Power. The creative or manifest aspect of Lord Shiva. His Divine energy which cannot be separated from Him. The underlying substrata of all existence, in its most refined aspect it is pure consciousness or ParaShakti, Satchitananda. Often depicted as individual entities, Shiva and Shakti are in fact inseparable like two sides of the same coin, or the dancer and the dance. See Ardhanarisvara.

Shaktipata: Descent of Grace, Guru Initiation. The awakening of the kundalini by a touch, look or thought.

Shanti: Peace.

Shiva (Siva): God, Absolute Reality (Parashiva), the Totality of Being existing in and as all things. The Creator and Creation, the preserver and destroyer. The supreme deity of the Shaivite (Saivite) religion.

Shivalingam: An ancient representation or symbol of Lord Shiva prevalent in many Hindu temples. Seed state consciousness.

Siddha Master: One who has gone beyond the siddhis - a Self-Realized or perfected master.

Siddhi: Extraordinary mystical or psychic powers arising as a result of sadhana or naturally through spiritual maturity. Often a barrier to Self-Realization due to the fortification of ego and the sense of separation. The ultimate or supreme siddhi is Realization of the Self or God.

Soham: I am Brahman.

Sri: Honorable, venerable, revered.

Tamas: *See* Gunas

Tantra/Tantric: Method. A specific method or spiritual practice which is used in every part of life to break through illusion. A mystical scripture or text.

Transient: That which is always in change and flux.

Upanishads: 108 spiritual and philosophical texts contained within the Vedas and from which Vedanta originates and expounding upon God, Creation and Cosmos.

Vairagya: Detachment

Vasanas: The subconscious inclinations which dictate ones attitudes and actions. When samskaras combine the resultant hybrids are vasanas.

Vedas: An immense four volume assembly of Holy Revelation. The foundation stone of Hinduism.

Vijnana: Special knowledge/spiritual knowledge.

Vipassana: Mindfulness mediation, watching ones thoughts and actions.

Yeshua: Christ.

Yoga: Union with the Divine, from the root verb 'to yoke'.

Yogas: Method of creation union. *See* Jnana Yoga, Bhaki Yoga, Karma Yoga).

Yoni mudra: Mudra to represent Shakti. Yoni – Shakti comes into existence. Lingam sits in Yoni.

Also available by Ganga Karmokar:

TRUTH UNBOUND
Pointings for the Path through Consciousness

Transcending Religion, Time and Bondage

Teachings pointing to the utter simplicity of Truth.
On Creation, Fear, Love, Compassion, the Self...

Published by Zen Way Center
ISBN 0-9777456-1-9

Currently available on request from:
zenwayadmin@hotmail.com.

Kundalini: From Hell to Heaven DVD/Video (includes footage of initiates with spontaneous kriyas)
* The Complete Satsang CDs (also available as downloads)
* Swami-G's sanyasi music

Contact information:
Kundalinisupport.com